VEGETATION OF
FRASER ISLAND / K'GARI

Includes a species list
of the flowering plants and ferns

Grahame Applegate
Illustrations and design by Bramita Andriana

Vegetation of Fraser Island / K'gari
Grahame Applegate
with illustrations and design by Bramita Andriana (petiterabbit.com)
ISBN 978-0-6488774-0-0
Published by
©2020 Grahame Applegate
1st Edition 2020

All photography by Grahame Applegate unless otherwise acknowledged

Ingram Book Company, October 2020

Cover Design: Design by Bramita Andriana, based on a painting of *Banksia robur* 2025, Artist Beryl Robertson.
The author is grateful for permission to use the painting.

FOREWORD

Fraser Island / K'gari together with the neighbouring Cooloola sand mass (on the Queensland mainland), makes up the Great Sandy biogeographical region. This unique area encompasses an almost one million-year-old series of giant Pleistocene and Holocene sand dunes, with a diverse array of plant communities ranging from sedgelands to tall open-forests and rainforests.

These latter forest communities provided a valuable source of timber from the early days of European settlement. Initially the rainforests were logged before attention turned to the wet sclerophyll forests dominated by brush box and the endemic giant turpentine or satinay (*Syncarpia hillii*). Satinay soon gained a reputation around the world for its endurance as a marine hardwood, e.g. in construction of the Suez Canal.

The adjacent tall eucalypt forests and particularly those dominated by blackbutt (*Eucalyptus pilularis*), have been an enduring and major timber resource until the relatively recent cessation of logging in the early 1990's. It was these forests which first brought Grahame Applegate to Fraser Island as a young research forester in 1979.

Although his career has since taken him to the rainforests of the Wet Tropics of North Queensland and then to various countries across South-East Asia and the Pacific, he has retained and now rekindled his personal and scientific fascination with the forests of the island following his return to the Sunshine Coast.

Although its outstanding natural values were recognised in its listing as Australia's eleventh World Heritage Area (in 1992) and despite its significance as a major tourist destination, there is little information available on the flora and fauna of Fraser Island. Detailed mapping of the plant communities has been available for more than 30 years, but this is the first published account of those communities and their ecological relationships. It also includes a comprehensive list of the plant species together with their habitats.

Dr W.J.F. (Bill) McDonald
Honorary Research Associate
Queensland Herbarium and
Queensland Parks and Wildlife Service

CONTENTS

LIST OF FIGURES

LIST OF TABLES

LIST OF PHOTOGRAPHS

PREFACE

This book evolved from the author's ecological research into the productivity of blackbutt forests on Fraser Island / K'gari.

For 18 months Grahame Applegate lived at the Central Station Field Laboratory, established on the island by the Queensland Forestry Department and the University of New England. As part of his research he established vegetation area plots in the forests and undertook detailed inventories of the plant species. The plots covered various growth stages of the blackbutt forests from saplings through to over-mature trees.

As Grahame gained a better appreciation of the island's natural beauty and surrounding waters, he wanted to understand the vegetation associations and the likely conditions which combined to create the often distinct, dynamic, vegetation types. How did the giants of Pile Valley, Yidney Scrub, the towering blackbutt forests, the natural kauri and hoop pine forests and the incredibly clear lakes with their white sandy beaches develop on an island that is mostly pure sand?

He expanded an early list of plant species of the blackbutt forests to include other vegetation associations on Fraser Island, with the assistance of the Queensland Herbarium staff. This formed part of a 1982 dissertation.

Grahame then moved to tropical forest management and plantation development and later, to researching peat fires and the subsequent restoration of the degraded peatlands in Indonesia.

On return to the Sunshine Coast in 2013, he joined the Tropical Forests and People Research Centre at the University of the Sunshine Coast. This was an opportunity to continue his earlier interest in Fraser Island / K'gari.

He revisited the forest plots, established jointly with the Queensland Forest Department 38 years earlier. He began to update and revise the original species list, which now includes more than 850 entries, noting many changes to species names which had occurred in the intervening years. Now, most of the island is gazetted as a National Park, gained World Heritage listing and the traditional owners, the Butchulla people, have gained Native Title landowner status.

One of the surprising findings on the island, as more species were identified and added to the list, was the huge increase in the number of invasive species. The late John Sinclair OA of FIDO often warned that this was going to be an issue as the island became more accessible to increasingly affordable 4WD vehicles. These vehicles precipitated a huge increase in annual visitor numbers with concomitant issues of erosion, accidental introduction of invasive species, overcrowding of scenic spots, beaches and roads.

Identifying the linkages between the vegetation types and the landforms in which they occur has been the main motivation for writing this book, as a way of sharing unique aspects of the island. The comprehensive list of flowering plants and fern species will enhance the enjoyment and understanding of the many, varied vegetation types on the island.

Grahame has used his detailed knowledge of the history, topography and vegetation of the island to design a route which the interested visitor can follow to explore the main floristic communities. He accompanies this with a narrative on places of historical and general interest along the inland roads and tracks.

This book is for the casual visitor and for those interested in the ecology to gain an appreciation of the uniqueness, variety and tenacity of the endemic plants, vegetation types and associations that Fraser Island / K'gari supports.

INTRODUCTION

Fraser Island / K'gari, lies in the Pacific Ocean close to the south-eastern coast of the Australian state of Queensland. It is the largest sand island in the world, covering an area of 166,000 ha[1]. Fraser Island / K'gari and the islands of Moreton Bay to the south, were formed in the Quaternary Period from onshore wind and littoral drift of shifting sands washed out of the coastal rivers which drained the highlands of south-east Queensland and northern New South Wales. The Cooloola sand mass on the mainland to the south and the coastal dune areas between the volcanic outcrops from Brisbane to Maryborough were formed simultaneously under the same climatic conditions.

Glacial periods and global changes in sea level affected the development of these islands, which are comprised almost entirely of siliceous sands. The northern beaches of Fraser Island / K'gari additionally have traces of calcareous material.

There are rocky headlands at Indian Head, Middle Rocks and Waddy Point, and other smaller outcrops that are comprised of consolidated cretaceous organic sand (coffee rock), occurring on exposed parts of the beaches on the east and west coast.

The island's narrow separation from the mainland during the Quaternary Period was caused by a rise in sea-level, which reached its approximate present level at the end of the ice age, about 6,000 years ago [2].

LOCATION

Fraser Island / K'gari lies between latitudes 24°41'S and 25°50' S and longitudes 152°55' E and 153°20' E. It is approximately 130 km long, 25 km at its widest point [3] and reaches a height of 244 metres above sea level (m a.s.l.). It lies generally in a NNE-SSW direction with its closest point to the mainland being less than 2 km at Hook Point in the south and more than 75 km at its most northerly point at Sandy Cape (Figure 1).

VEGETATION

A mosaic of vegetation types covers the island and is determined mainly by topography, hydrology, dune age, soil type, fire and the degree of exposure.

The soils that support this large range of vegetation types generally are deep, uniformly textured sands with some duplex soils and acid peats in the numerous swamps located close to the east and west coasts.

The vegetation includes closed forests dominated by rainforest species, found in many protected parts in the centre of the island. Inland areas feature open forests dominated by tall trees from the Myrtaceae family (*Eucalyptus pilularis, Eucalyptus microcorys, Lophostemon confertus, Syncarpia hillii, Angophora leiocarpa*). Wallum communities, including *Banksia* spp. and *Callitris columellaris* (cypress pine) thrive on the western older dunes. Eight mangrove species are found in the intertidal areas and salt marshes along the west coast.

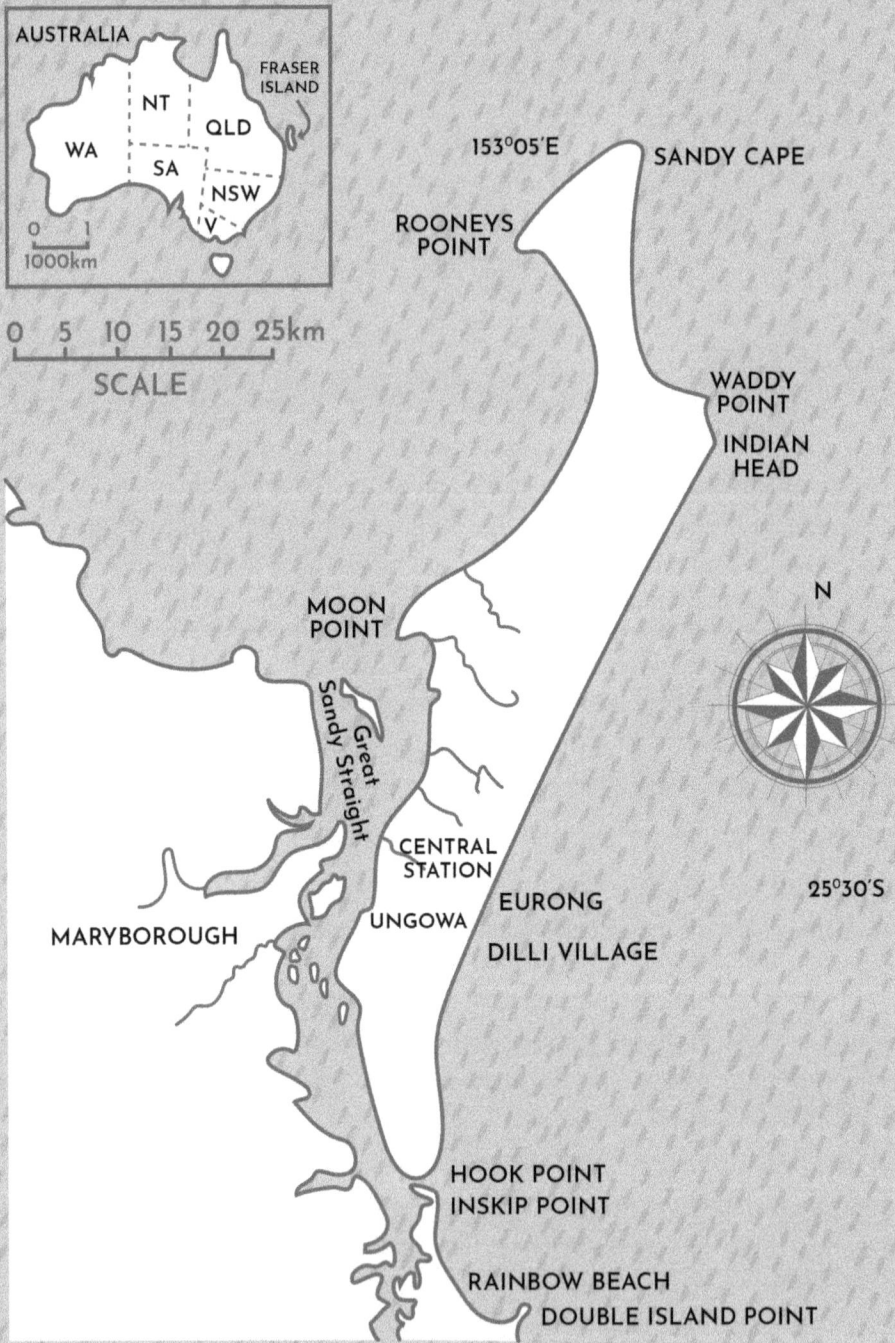

FIGURE 1: Location map of Fraser Island / K'gari.

AUSTRALIA

FRASER ISLAND

NT

QLD

WA

SA

NSW

V

0   1
1000km

0   5   10   15   20 25km

SCALE

153°05'E

SANDY CAPE

ROONEYS
POINT

WADDY
POINT

INDIAN
HEAD

MOON
POINT

N

Great
Sandy Straight

CENTRAL
STATION

EURONG

25°30'S

UNGOWA

MARYBOROUGH

DILLI VILLAGE

HOOK POINT
INSKIP POINT

RAINBOW BEACH
DOUBLE ISLAND POINT

CLIMATE

Fraser Island / K'gari has a subtropical climate with moderate temperatures and local variations across the island that roughly follow the topography and vegetation types.

Mean maximum temperatures recorded for Sandy Cape on the northern part of the island range from 28.6 °C in January (summer) to 20.7 °C in July (winter). Large changes between night and day temperatures can be experienced in the centre of the island, where frosts may occur in winter and summer temperatures often exceed 35.0 °C.

Seasonal rain falls mostly between December and May and is often associated with cyclones.

The eastern side and central part of the island usually receive between 1,500 mm and 1,600 mm/year (Eurong 1,567 mm and Central Station 1,550 mm). The long-term annual average at Sandy Cape Lighthouse is 1,268 mm recorded over a period of 145 years [4]. Rainfall recordings for Ungowa on the west coast show an annual average of 1,740 mm. The highest dunes in the centre of the island probably receive about 1,800 mm annually [5].

The winds are predominantly from the south-east with some north-easterly winds in summer and westerly and south-westerly winds in winter. Cyclones regularly affect the island between November and March, causing damage to the vegetation of varying magnitude.

GROUND WATER

Beneath the permeable sands, the underground water surface maintains a natural dome shape, sloping towards the west and east coasts from the centre of the island at a gradient of about 1:100. Reputed to be the world's largest unconfined aquifer on a sand island, often this water is seen flowing across the beaches on the east and west coasts.

Lake Boomanjin, one of the numerous lakes on the island, is an example of an area that has previously experienced higher water tables, where the water pooled in depressions lined with cemented sand grains, decaying vegetation (organic matter) and iron particles [6]. This resulted in a non-permeable zone ('hard pan') that remained after the water table subsided. These lakes are now separate from, or above, the main water table and often are referred to as perched lakes [6]. Window lakes occur where the water table rises above the ground surface and remains high. Large seasonal fluctuations occur in the level of the window lakes as the water table rises and falls. However, water levels in the perched lakes are determined by relationships between rainfall, evaporation and internal seepage patterns [7]. Generally, the maximum depth of the lakes is less than 10 metres. Lake Boorangoora (also known as Lake McKenzie) is one of the most well-known of the perched lakes and receives thousands of visitors annually. Lake Wabby is the deepest lake at 11.4 metres. Most of the lakes are not thermally stratified and their pH ranges from 4.2 to 6 [8]. The lakes have a low salinity, approximately 40 mg/l, dominated by sodium and chlorine, with the relative proportions of the major inorganic elements similar to those of the surrounding sea water [8][9].

GEOLOGY AND SOILS

The island consists almost entirely of unconsolidated quartzose sand, sitting above predominantly sedimentary Cretaceous Period rocks (138 million years old). The recent Quaternary Period (less than 1.6 million years old), produced dune and beach sands that lie on top of the Cretaceous rocks which extend down to about 30 metres [3]. Gravel and river sand have been recorded as well as Quaternary sand above the Cretaceous rocks. These Mesozoic Era rocks are probably Maryborough Basin formations overlying the trachytic flows of the Graham's Creek Formation, overtopping the Palaeozoic Era basement rock [6].

The rocky outcrops on the eastern side of the island correlate with the Oligocene Age and consist of grey trachytic volcanic lavas with beds and lenses of agglomerate, about 25 million years old [10]. Waddy Point is made up of mid-Tertiary trachytic lava with basalt dykes and zones of agglomerate. Middle Rocks is similar in composition to Waddy Point, while Indian Head is composed of trachyte with large scale columnar jointing up to 10 metres in height exhibited on the northern face.

Cherts formed from silicified, fossiliferous, marine mudstone of the Maryborough Basin rocks are seen at Bun Bun Rocks on the west coast. These cherts belong to the lower Cretaceous Period.

The soils which have developed on the beach and dunes are variable and tend to occur in a mosaic which is influenced by the age of the dune, topography, the level of the water table, and past and present climate.

Generally, the soils can be characterised as podzols. They have a thin 0 horizon (layer), a thick, dark organic A1 horizon, a bleached thick A2 horizon and a B horizon of varying depth and thickness. The B horizon is composed of accumulated organic, iron and aluminium compounds, often reddish in colour [11].

In areas where the water table has reached, the soil weathering zone forms humus podzols, while peat (organic soil) has developed in the swamps and shallow lakes.

A map of Fraser Island / K'gari place names is shown in Figure 2.

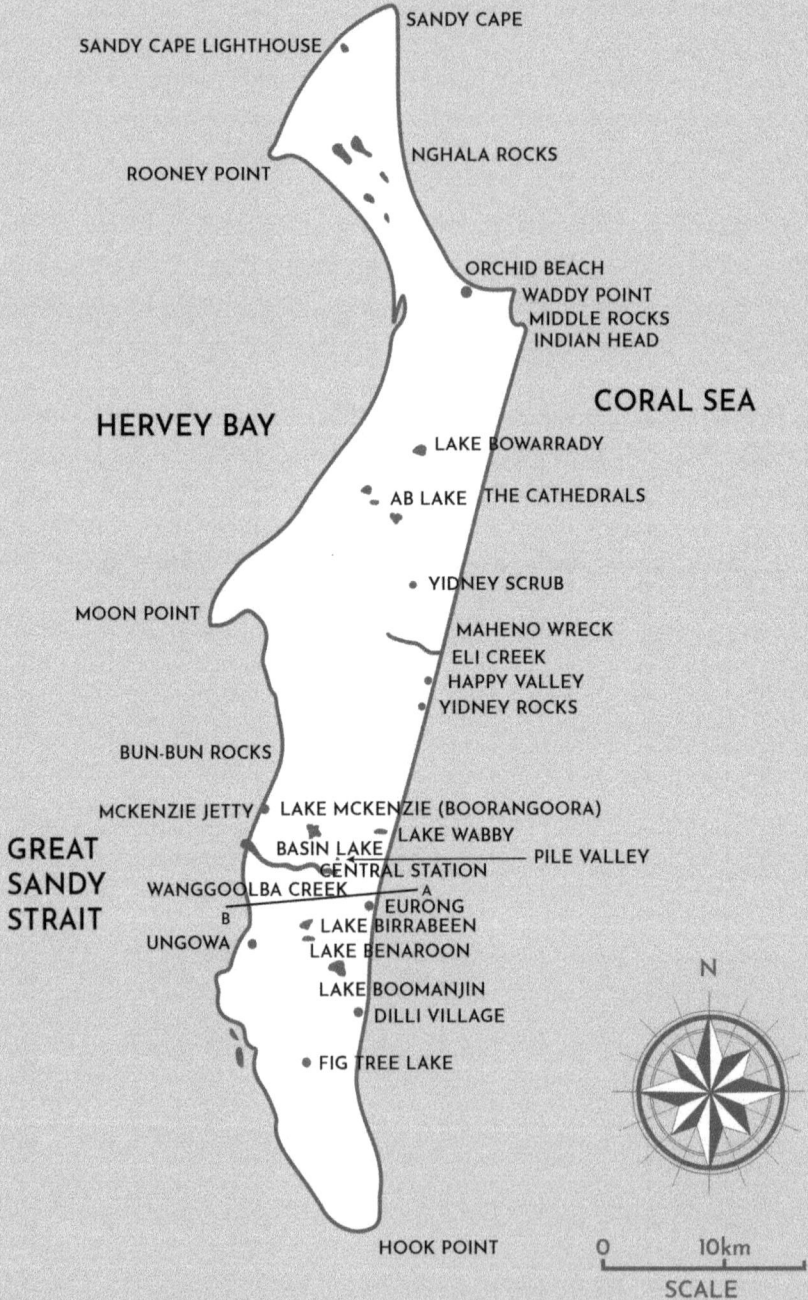

FIGURE 2: Location map of Fraser Island / K'gari showing place names.

GEOMORPHOLOGY

The island's sands originated from extensive sandstone deposits in New South Wales; the result of weathering and transportation of the sand sediment into the ocean, followed by a northward littoral migration [6][12].

These sands (located as much as 60 metres below current sea levels) were blown towards the island by the predominant south-easterly winds during the Quaternary Period [13]. Wave action brought the sand on to the beaches during periods when the sea rose at the end of the last ice age.

Hence, Fraser Island / K'gari comprises dune sands (wind deposited sand) and beach sands (wave deposited sand) most of which have a parabolic form with trailing edges that lie parallel to the dominant south-east trade winds. In the north of the island however, the dunes show a landform of broad, wave-shaped ridges, some of which are at right angles to the prevailing winds.

The boundary between the younger coastal plain dune sand and beach sand landforms formed in the Quaternary Period are noticeable. The older Pleistocene sand dunes in the middle and western side of the island have degraded, losing much of their original wind-formed topography and are more difficult to identify [6]. The old sands that extend back into the early Pleistocene Period, sometimes contain small amounts of silt and clay.

DUNE AGE

The age of some dunes has been calculated from glacial periods, shorelines dated elsewhere and from the degree of weathering and soil development [6]. The well-drained, continuously exposed sand dunes have been leached and undergone podsolization. This leaves white sand overlying sands stained various colours with the products from the leaching [13] . (These 'coloured sands' are similar to those seen on parts of the east coast and at Cooloola near Rainbow Beach on the mainland.)

The thickness of the leached zone (to subsoil B horizon) increases with the age of the depositional unit, providing a useful guide to dune age [14][15]. There is an equivalent decline in fertility and, in the older dunes, this is evidenced by sparse and low vegetative cover as is common on parts of the west coast.

Nine major phases of dune sand accumulations have been recorded. The oldest being on the western side of the island. During the Holocene Period, three major sets of dune sands appeared and, unlike the other six, were derived from sand below sea level [14].

The distinction between beach sands is made on geological grounds and include criteria such as degree of soil profile development (depth to the B horizon) and differences related to sea level changes.

Table 1 shows the approximate ages since formation of the dune and beach sands. During the last glacial period (42,000 to 10,000 years ago), the Triangle Cliff Dune Sand was formed during the Pleistocene Period when the sea level was low. It is likely that all sand units deposited subsequent to this are less than 10,000 years old, i.e. formed in the Holocene Period.

The Ungowa, Poyungan and Wathumba Beach Sand formations were formed approximately 400,000, 330,000 and 75,000, years ago respectively [16]. No dunes were formed from 75,000 to 100,000 years ago which suggests the winds in the inter-glacial period were only slight.

	DUNE SAND	BEACH SAND	AGE (YEARS)
HOLOCENE		Modern	< 150
	Modern		< 150
		Hook	300
	Cape		800
		Rooney Point	2,000
	Station Hill		3,000
		Bool Creek	5,000
PLEISTOCENE	Triangle Cliff		10,000–7,000
		Wathumba	7,000–5,000
	Garrawongera		40,000
		Woorim	75,000
		No dunes formed	
		Brible	100,000
	Bowarrady		250,000
		Poyungan	330,000
	Yankee Jack		350,000
		Ungowa	400,000
	Awinya		500,000

TABLE 1: Age of Beach Sand and Dune Sand accumulations on Fraser Island / K'gari.

Sand accumulations have coincided with climatic changes in the past. The ice age caused the sea level to drop, while the interglacial period caused it to rise. The period of dune sand formation occurred during the glacial period when a large wide beach was created by the drop in sea level. The action of the associated south-east winds then built up and shaped the dunes in a similar manner as seen today in the bare sandy regions on the eastern side of the island.

The beach sand formations built up during interglacial periods when the sea level rose, caused the strands to develop in the tidal zone, as they do today [10]. The three recent dune sand building episodes occurred when the sea level approximated that of today and were short lived. These younger soils can be classified as siliceous sands or podzols. On low ground, where ground water levels are high, humus podzols have developed. The depth to the B horizon of these younger Holocene Period deposits can be to half a metre, whereas the oldest deposits can extend to 13 metres [10]. The windy conditions required for such formations could have occurred during the so-called 'Little Ice Age' in post glacial times and explain the formation of these dunes as shown in Figure 3.

FIGURE 3: Location of the Beach and Dune Sand accumulations on Fraser Island / K'gari.

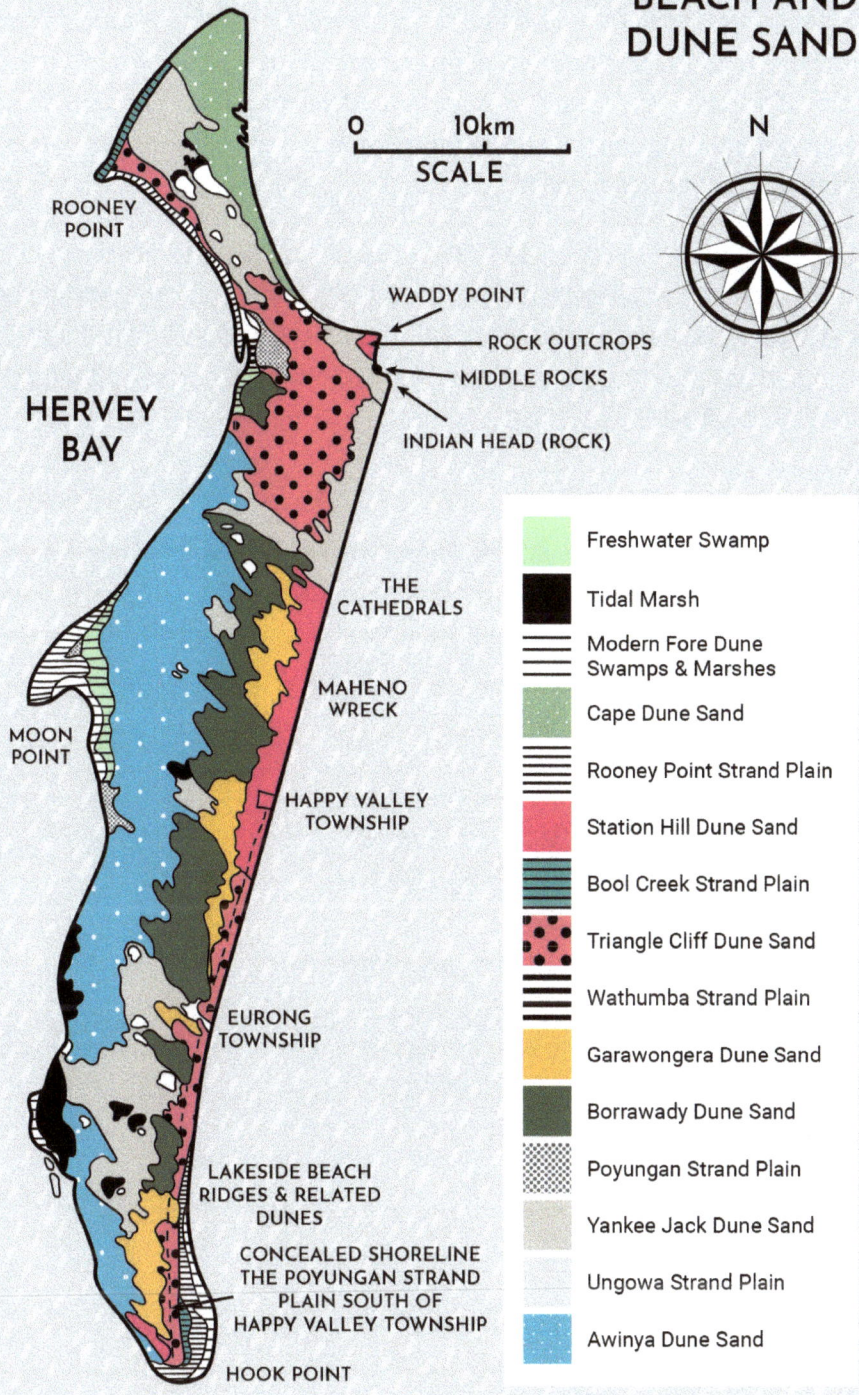

BEACH AND DUNE SAND

ROONEY
POINT

HERVEY
BAY

WADDY POINT

ROCK OUTCROPS

MIDDLE ROCKS

INDIAN HEAD (ROCK)

THE
CATHEDRALS

MAHENO
WRECK

MOON
POINT

HAPPY VALLEY
TOWNSHIP

EURONG
TOWNSHIP

LAKESIDE BEACH
RIDGES & RELATED
DUNES

CONCEALED SHORELINE
THE POYUNGAN STRAND
PLAIN SOUTH OF
HAPPY VALLEY TOWNSHIP

HOOK POINT

0   10km
SCALE

N

	Freshwater Swamp
	Tidal Marsh
	Modern Fore Dune Swamps & Marshes
	Cape Dune Sand
	Rooney Point Strand Plain
	Station Hill Dune Sand
	Bool Creek Strand Plain
	Triangle Cliff Dune Sand
	Wathumba Strand Plain
	Garawongera Dune Sand
	Borrawady Dune Sand
	Poyungan Strand Plain
	Yankee Jack Dune Sand
	Ungowa Strand Plain
	Awinya Dune Sand

12

Reworking of the sand is due largely to wind erosion, often resulting in the formation of blowouts or sand blows. Sand blows are common on the eastern coastline. Fore dunes have developed on the north-western shores of many lakes. They are associated with water level fluctuations and prevailing south-easterly winds. In some places their topographies were altered by blowouts in the sand dunes caused by wind [10][17].

Reworking of the deposits by the sea results in fine sediments and muds, seen on the western shores where wave energy is low. On the eastern shoreline, high energy wave action and the prevailing south-easterly winds result in rapid, longshore, sand drift, as seen in the long sandy shoals that extend far to the north of Sandy Cape [15].

DEPOSITION UNITS

Fraser Island, Moreton Island, Stradbroke Island and Cooloola, were formed under similar conditions and have related geomorphology or physiography. Consequently, their sand formations can be considered together in five broad categories or deposition units as [18]:

1. Old White Sand
2. Coloured or Teewah Sands
3. High Transgressive Sand Dunes
4. Yellow Brown Transgressive Sand Dunes
5. Low Sand Dune and Fore Dune Complex

DUNE UNITS (LANDSCAPE CLASSIFICATION)

Initially, the dunes were classified using a landscape approach [5]. The Dune Unit boundaries are closely aligned with the depositional classification based on Geological Units as shown in Table 2 [6].

DUNE UNIT	GEOLOGICAL UNIT
Hook	Modern Beach Sand, Modern Dune Sand, Hook Beach Sand, Cape Dune Sand, Rooney Point Beach Sand, Station Hill Dune Sand, Bool Creek Beach Sand
Moon Point	Rooney Point Beach Sand, Bool Creek Beach Sand, Wathumba Beach Sand, Poyungan Beach Sand
Panama	Modern Beach Sand
Puthoo	Modern Beach Sand
Wathumba	Modern Beach Sand, Wathumba Beach Sand, Poyungan Beach Sand
Boomanjin	Yankee Jack Dune Sand
Ngala	Cape Dune Sand
Station Creek	Station Hill Dune Sand, Modern Beach Sand
Bool Creek	Bool Creek Beach Sand
Eurong	Triangle Cliff Dune Sand
Waddy	Triangle Cliff Dune Sand
Eli	Hill Dune Sand, Triangle Cliff Dune Sand
Bogimbah	Garrawongera Dune Sand, Bowarrady Dune Sand, Yankee Jack Dune Sand
Ungowa	Awinya Dune Sand
Krambruk	Yankee Jack Dune Sand
Boomerang	Awinya Dune Sand
Cathedrals	Station Hill Dune Sand
Markwell	Rooney Point Strand Plain, Triangle Cliff Dune Sand, Bool Creek Strand Plain

TABLE 2: Relationship between Dune Units (Soil Landscape) and Geological Units on Fraser Island / K'gari.

PHYSIOGRAPHIC UNITS

The dunes can be classified further according to their physiography or landform. The physiographic units have been given habitat names to allow easy identification and to enable a better understanding of where particular vegetation types occur. The names and descriptions of the physiographic units are outlined as follows:

STRAND

This area comprises beach and dune sand and extends up to a height of approximately 5 metres above sea level. It includes the first berm (sand ridge) and small seepage areas above the high-water mark.

FORE DUNE

Situated immediately behind the Strand, the Fore Dunes extend up to 20 metres in height. They include the second berm and larger seepage areas such as swales (shallow depressions), creeks and lagoons.

HIND DUNE

This unit comprises the series of parabolic dunes (with a trailing edge) which extend up to a height of 80 metres above sea level and up to three kilometres inland. The soils on these sands are usually yellow/brown with little organic matter in the surface layers.

HIGH DUNE

Much of the central part of the island can be classified as High Dune. These contain most of the better developed forests which include the *Eucalyptus pilularis* (blackbutt) dominated forests, satinay-brush box forests and rainforests (closed forest). Also found here are many of the lakes and lake infills containing peat that dot the island.

LITTORAL FLATS

These are found on the western side of the island and include mangrove woodlands, salt marshes and the transition zone between the marsh lands and the forests on the dune sands. Most are inundated at high tide with intermittent covering of the transition zone occurring at High Water Springs.

FLORISTIC ENVIRONMENT

GENERAL RELATIONSHIPS

Plant formations on the island often are separated from one another by clearly visible narrow boundaries, such as varying heights and species. The factors largely responsible for determining the type of vegetation are

1. Depth to water table
2. Soil age (depth to B Horizon)
3. Topography and nearness to the ocean
4. History and frequency of events such as fires and cyclones.

WATER TABLE AND VEGETATION

Many of the island habitats of different vegetation formations are closely related to water table depth. The water tables range from those seen in permanent free water (lakes, streams and soakage areas), on poorly drained flat lands, to hills of sand where the water table is permanently below the ground surface. Additionally, mangrove communities in intertidal and upstream areas on the west coast develop on substrates where wave energy is low compared to the ocean-fronted eastern coastline.

In areas of permanent free water, plants establish on the surrounding terrestrial edge and to several metres below the surface. Typically, few aquatic plant species occur in the lakes.

TOPOGRAPHY AND VEGETATION

The plant formations occurring on the flat lands and low rises form what is known generally as 'wallum country'.

Wallum was the name given to some species of banksia by the Aborigines of south-eastern Queensland. The term 'wallum country' has been adopted for coastal plains where these plants are common [19].

The vegetation formations vary from closed-sedgeland (dominated by the Restionaceae), to (closed-) open-heath (mixtures of families represented) on the lowest lying ground, to open-scrub or low open-forests containing *Banksia* and/or *Eucalyptus* spp. on the low rises.

The structural classification of the vegetation types follows that developed by Dr Specht in 1970 [20].

The sandy hills on the remainder of the island are dominated by four main vegetation types. These consist of formations dominated by:

1. *Eucalyptus racemosa* (scribbly gum)
2. *Eucalyptus pilularis* (blackbutt)
3. *Syncarpia hillii* (satinay/Fraser satinay or turpentine) and *Lophostemon confertus* (brush box)
4. Rainforest species.

GEOLOGY – SAND DEPOSITION – PHYSIOGRAPHY – LANDSCAPE

There is a strong relationship between geology, soil, physiography and vegetation. The vegetation exhibits a mosaic pattern, often with sharply defined boundaries between the different plant communities. The nature of these boundaries is dependent largely on the interaction of the soil (dune age), nutrient status, water table depth, fire and physiography. These relationships have evolved over time, resulting in distinct physiographic boundaries (Physiographic Unit). These correlate with the sand deposits (Depositional Unit), geology (Geological Unit) and the Dune Unit, as shown in Table 3.

GEOLOGICAL UNIT	DEPOSITIONAL UNIT	PHYSIOGRAPHIC UNIT	DUNE UNIT
Modern Beach Sand (<150 yrs)	Beach–Fore Dune	Strand (0 m–5 m a.s.l.)	Eurong
Triangle Cliff Dune Sand (10,000–7,000 yrs)	Low Undulating Sand Dune Complex	Fore Dune- 2nd berm (5 m–20 m a.s.l.) (seepage areas, creeks and lagoons)	Eurong
Triangle Cliff Dune Sand (10,000–7,000 yrs) Bowarrady Dune Sand (250,000 yrs)	Low Yellow/Brown Transgressive Sand Dune	Hind Dune (20 m–80 m a.s.l.)	Eli, Markwell
Garrawongera Dune Sand (40,000 yrs) Bowarrady Dune Sand (250,000 yrs) Yankee Jack Dune Sand (350,000 yrs)	High Transgressive Sand Dune	High Dune (80 m–140 m a.s.l.)	Bogimbah, Boomanjin
Awinya Dune Sand (500,000 yrs)	Old White Sands	High Dune (2 m–80 m a.s.l.)	Ungowa, Panama
Tidal Marsh (recent)	Littoral Flats	Littoral Flats (0 m–2 m a.s.l.)	Panama
Station Hill Dune Sand (3,000–2,000 yrs) Triangle Cliff Dune Sand (10,000–7,000 yrs)	Coloured Sands (Teewah)	Steep/Deeply Eroded Dune	Cathedral

TABLE 3: Relationship between the Geological, Depositional and Physiographic and Dune Units.

SOIL AGE – DEPTH OF LEACHING – VEGETATION

The relationships between soil age, depth of leaching (B Horizon) and vegetation types are very strong and influenced by topography, itself being influenced by duration of exposure to weathering.

Generally, the *Eucalyptus pilularis* (open forest) dominated forests occur on well drained, medium-aged to old sand dunes. The rainforests (closed forest) occur on similar dunes but in better protected locations. *Eucalyptus racemosa* dominated forests occur on both young and old dunes, while the wallum communities tend to be on the oldest dunes of low relief. The most extensive wallum communities occur on the western side of the island. The relationship between depth to B horizon in sand podzols, age of deposition and distribution of vegetation types is shown in Figure 4 [21].

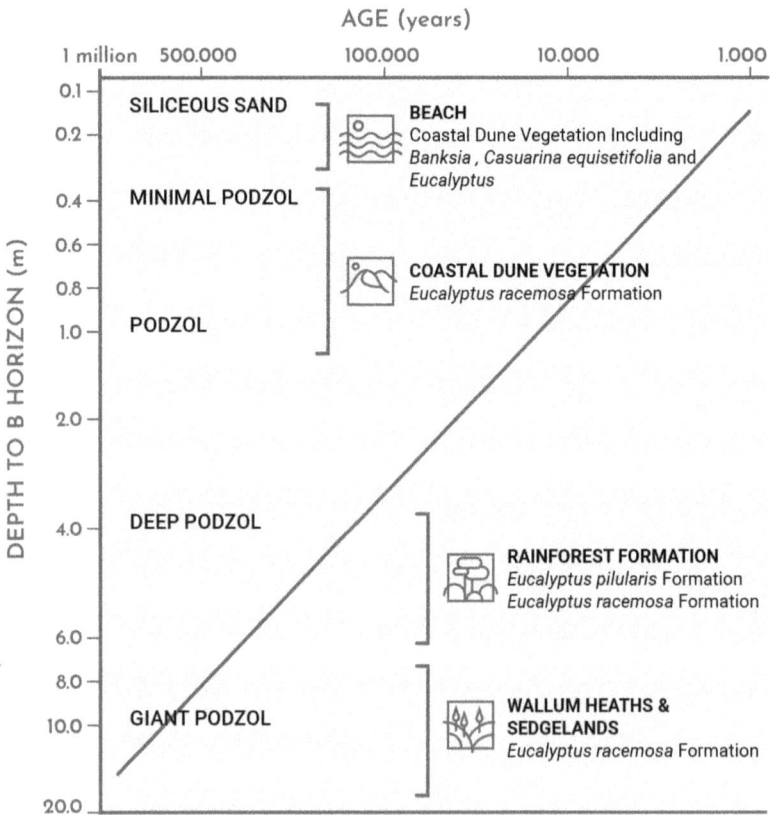

FIGURE 4: Relationship between depth to B horizon in sand podzols, age of deposition and distribution of vegetation type on Fraser Island / K'gari.

EXPOSURE AND PROXIMITY TO THE OCEAN

Exposure to the prevailing winds greatly influences the nature of the vegetation, particularly on the eastern coastline. Fore Dune communities dominated by *Spinifex sericeus* may be depleted or destroyed annually by erosion during periods of high wave activity, such as during the cyclone season.

The zonation of species groupings perpendicular to the beach varies with the intensity of exposure and rates of accretion or depletion of the sand.

Additionally, species occurring in dune communities (*Acacia* spp., *Banksia* spp.) may be subjected to pruning and 'burning' of the young growing tips by salt-laden winds blowing off the ocean.

FIRE

Fire is a common environmental factor in all of the vegetation communities except those dominated by rainforest species. Fires are seldom seen in the rainforests today, but most likely occurred in these same locations in the past.

The over-story tree species (*Syncarpia hillii* and *Lophostemon confertus*) seen often in the rainforests today, are the direct result of much earlier fires or major disturbances, hundreds of years ago.

Fire events have probably been a factor in the regeneration of many plant communities for thousands of years [22]. Over the past 24,000 years fire has generally been of low frequency with low return intervals [23].

In the past 350 to 600 years, the vegetation in many parts of the island was predominantly closed forest with emergent species such as *Araucaria cunninghamii, Agathis robusta, Podocarpus elatus* and Myrtaceous vegetation. Today these are confined mostly to the sheltered central parts of the island [24].

Captain Cook noted in 1770 when sailing past the island, that the Aboriginal communities had fires burning in the heaths and low open forests [25]. These are the vegetation communities surrounding the more developed tall open and closed forests. The extent of the vegetation communities today is different from those in the recent past. These successions are due to climatic changes, different fire regimes (natural events and anthropogenic causes) and weather events [24].

Changes in fire intensity and frequency have caused changes to the vegetation types and to the species composition within vegetation types, with some species adapted to regular fires becoming inconspicuous in the absence of regular burns. *Blandfordia grandiflora*, (Christmas bells) a ground orchid once conspicuous in the wallum, has disappeared from many areas where fire regimes have changed in recent years.

Although the frequency and extent of recent fires were not recorded formally on the island prior to 1952, the frequency of fire within the wet sclerophyll forest types, such as the satinay-brush box forests, is much less than in drier sclerophyll blackbutt dominated forests.

The sclerophyll vegetation, such as those in the wallum, usually experience annual periods of water stress associated with greater flammability. Periods of high flammability in wet sclerophyll areas (satinay-brush box forests) occur, but less often, as evidenced by the scorch marks seen on the boles of many large *Syncarpia* trees.

In general, the sclerophyll vegetation (as in much of Australia) is dominated by the family Myrtaceae, particularly *Eucalyptus* spp. The majority of eucalypts are resistant to fire. For many, the outer bark may be severely burnt whilst the cambium and concealed buds are protected, later forming green epicormic shoots along the trunk and branches. Additionally, many species form lignotubers from which new shoots develop following the destruction of the above-ground parts of the tree.

Eucalyptus pilularis has neither of these two capabilities for resisting fires. Its bark is mostly thin, its seedlings are not resistant to fire and the older trees are able to resist moderate fires only. However, the species usually produces large amounts of fruit and following a fire, a heavy seed fall can be expected for regeneration by seedlings [26]. These characteristics were well recognised by early foresters who used 'regeneration burns' after logging in some areas to promote this highly desirable species.

Many of the large trees in the *Eucalyptus pilularis* dominated forests seen in the central regions of the island today are the result of medium to hot fires in the past, either from 'regeneration burns' or wildfires.

RARE AND THREATENED FLORA

Species on Fraser Island / K'gari which have been identified as being under threat include: *Acacia baueri* subsp. *baueri, Archidendron lovelliae, Blandfordia grandiflora, Boronia rivularis, Cinnamomum baileyanum, Diteilis (Liparis) simmondsii, Macrozamia pauli-quilielmi, Persoonia prostrata, Phaius australis, Syncarpia hillii* and *Tecomanthe hillii* [27]. Some species are relatively isolated (disjunct) from their other populations and therefore of regional importance and include: *Angiopteris evecta, Ripogonum discolor, Harpullia alata, Polyscias australiana, Lindsaea repens, Pitaviaster haplophyllus* and *Phaleria chermsideana.*

It is worth noting that there are some species which are confined to the island or have limited ranges on the mainland. These species include: *Archidendron lovelliae, Macrozamia douglasii, Myrsine arenicola, Syncarpia hillii,* and *Tecomanthe hillii.* The vegetation type commonly called satinay-brush box, a tall closed / open forest, is well developed on the island but absent from the mainland. If it is present on other sand islands close by, it is mainly in the form of small trees or mallee formations.

Fraser Island / K'gari is a place where some tree species reach their northern geographic range. Species in this category include: *Eucalyptus pilularis* (found only in the lower two-thirds of the island), *Corymbia gummifera* and *Eucalyptus racemosa.* Similarly, *Melaleuca quinquenervia* dominates open forest/woodland near to the northern limit of its distribution and naturally occurring hoop pine (*Araucaria cunninghamii*) is confined to the middle section of the island.

PEAT SWAMPS

The peat swamps are fens which are approximately 6,000 years old, amongst the oldest in the world and were first recorded and documented in 1996 [28] [29]. These 'patterned fens' or wetlands are unique as they occur only at subtropical latitudes, where decomposition rates are much higher than fens in much cooler climates.

Fens form on undecomposed plant material (peat) and are described as peat-forming wetlands. They obtain nutrients through drainage from upland mineral soils and groundwater movement. They support diverse plant communities such as grasses, sedges, rushes, herbs and shrubs [30].

The island's fens were formed almost at sea level and merge on the western side with mangrove forests. They are the only known examples of fens flowing into tidal wetlands anywhere in the world.

The patterned fens are mainly 'string fens' which form a striking and intricate maze of pools intersected by peat ridges (strings) of different thicknesses, rather than being patterns within the vegetation community with which they are associated. They are formed at the base of higher dunes where there is a constant and high flow of surface freshwater [31]. The pools which form become progressively deeper, reaching up to 1.5 metres in depth and are linked to small sandy streams.

VEGETATION ASSOCIATIONS

VEGETATION AND PHYSIOGRAPHY

The structure and vegetation types form broad patterns, lying sequentially from east to west, based on soils, (age of dune), water table and physiography.

The central part of the island contains many of the vegetation associations found throughout other locations on Fraser Island / K'gari. The vegetation types as shown in Table 4, reveal how closely related the various compositional processes are to each other. The physiography is a feature of the landscape which correlates closely with the geology, sand depositional age and vegetation type. Thus, the physiographic units, described previously are used to assist to classify the location of the vegetation types which follow the structural classification developed by Dr Specht in 1970 [20].

Broad Vegetation Groups (BVGs) are high-level groupings of vegetation communities, developed by the Queensland Herbarium [32]. Broad Vegetation Groups provide an overview of vegetation communities across the state or bioregion and allow comparison with other states in Australia. A description of the BVGs which are found on the island and their codes are provided in Appendix 1.

Table 4 shows the relationship between the physiography, the structural form of the vegetation and the Broad Vegetation Groups.

PHYSIOGRAPHIC UNIT	VEGETATION STRUCTURAL FORM	BVG CODE	DUNE LAND
Strand	Grassland–Sedgeland–Herbland	34c	Eurong, Hook, Cathedral, Ngkala
Fore Dune	Sedgeland–Low Woodland–Low Open Forest (seepage areas/ creeks, shallow & deep)	28c	Eurong
Hind Dune	Woodland–Open Forest	9g	Eli
High Dune Higher Dune–Ridges Higher Dune–Lower Slopes	Open Forest–Tall Open Forest	8a, 8b	Bogimbah
(a) Flats	Open Heath–Low Open Forest	28d, 29a	Ungowa
(b) Swamps/Lakes	Sedgeland–Woodland	34a (lakes), 34c	Boomanjin
(c) Valleys	Closed Forest–Tall Forest	3a, 4a	Bogimbah
Lower Dune–Ridges Lower Dune–Lower Slopes	Woodland–Open Forest	9g	Boomerang
(a) Flats	Closed Heath–Open Forest	29a	Ungowa
(b) Valleys	Low Woodland–Low Open Forest	22a	Ungowa
Littoral Flats	Low Open Forest–Woodland– Grassland	35a mangroves	Panama, Puthoo, Station Hill, Bool Creek, Moon Point
	Sedgeland–Herbland	35b	Wathumba

TABLE 4: Relationship between Physiography, Vegetation (Structural Form), BVG Units and Dune Lands on Fraser Island / K'gari.

Figure 5 depicts the main sand dune systems and their age, along with the physiographic units and the vegetation types in the form of an east-west cross-section (A-B) of the island passing through Central Station.

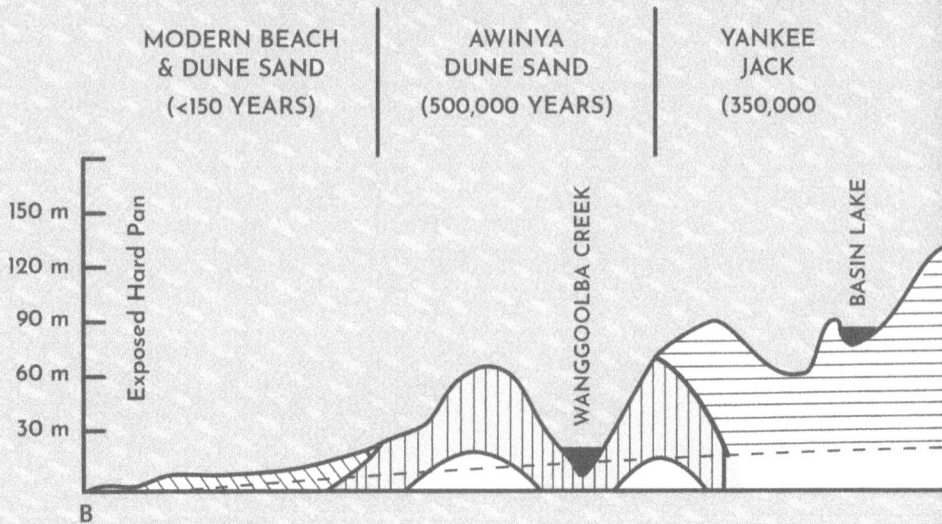

	MODERN BEACH & DUNE SAND (<150 YEARS)	AWINYA DUNE SAND (500,000 YEARS)	YANKEE JACK (350,000
DEPOSITIONAL UNIT	Littoral Flats & Dunes	Old White Sands	High Transgressive Dunes
DUNE LAND	Panama, Bool & Rooney Dune Land	Ungowa Dune Land	Bogimbah Dune Land
PHYSIOGRAPHIC UNIT	Littoral Flats (0–2 m a.s.l.)	High Dune–lower (2–80 m a.s.l.)	High Dune (80–240 m a.s.l.)
STRUCTURAL UNIT	Grassland–Herbland Low Woodland Woodland	Woodland Open Forest	Sedgeland–Heathland Forest–Tall Open Forest Closed–Tall Closed Forest
SPECIES	Aegialitis annulata	Banksia integrifolia	Agathis robusta
	Aegiceras corniculatum	Banksia robur	Baloskion tetraphyllum
	Avicennia marina	Blandfordia grandiflora	Baumea rubiginosa
	Ceriops australis	Callitris columellaris	Boronia falcifolia
	Excoecaria agallocha	Eucalyptus robusta	Drosera spatulata
	Hibiscus tiliaceus	Eucalyptus tereticornis	Dodonaea triquetra
	Lumnitzera racemosa	Eucalyptus racemosa	Endiandra sieberi
	Osbornia octodonta	Leptospermum spp.	Elaeocarpus grandis
	Rhizophora stylosa	Melaleuca quinquenervia	Eucalyptus pilularis
	Sesuvium portulacastrum	Ricinocarpos pinifolius	Eucalyptus resinifera
	Suaeda arbusculoides	Passiflora pallida	Gahnia sieberiana

FIGURE 5: Cross- section (AB) of Fraser Island through Central Station showing the relationship between the Depositional, Dune and Physiographic Units and the Vegetation Structural Forms.

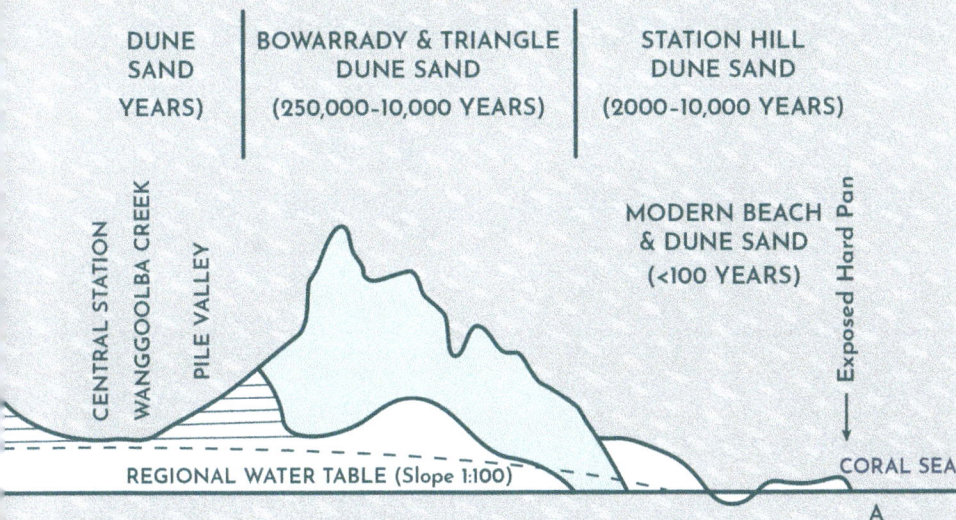

DUNE SAND YEARS)

BOWARRADY & TRIANGLE DUNE SAND (250,000-10,000 YEARS)

STATION HILL DUNE SAND (2000-10,000 YEARS)

CENTRAL STATION

WANGGOOLBA CREEK

PILE VALLEY

MODERN BEACH & DUNE SAND (<100 YEARS)

Exposed Hard Pan

CORAL SEA

A

REGIONAL WATER TABLE (Slope 1:100)

Low Yellow/Brown Transgressive Dunes	Undulating Low Dunes	Beach Fore Dunes
Eli Dune Land	Eurong Dune Land	Eurong Dune Land
Hind Dune (20–80 m a.s.l.)	Fore Dune (5–20 m a.s.l.)	Strand (0–5 m a.s.l.)
Woodland Open Forest	Low Woodland Low–Open Forest	Grassland Sedgeland Herbland
Laxmannia gracilis	Acacia falciformis	Bacopa monnieri	Carex pumila
Lepidosperma longitudinale	Alphitonia excelsa	Carpobrotus glaucescens	Digitaria leucostachya
Lepironia articulata	Angophora costata	Centella asiatica	Eleocharis equisetina
Lophostemon confertus	Banksia aemula	Eleocharis difformis	Ficinia nodosa
Oberonia palmicola	Casuarina glauca	Nymphoides exiliflora	Fimbristylis nutans
Pimelea linifolia	Corymbia tessellaris	Oenothera drummondii	Ipomoea pes-caprae
Platycerium bifurcatum	Eucalyptus racemosa	Pandanus tectorius	Lobelia alata
Schoenus brevifolius	Eucalyptus siderophloia	Philydrum lanuginosum	Philydrum lanuginosum
Syncarpia hillii	Macrozamia douglasii	Spinifex sericeus	Poranthera microphylla
Syzygium luehmannii	Persoonia virgata	Triglochin striata	Utricularia lateriflora
Xyris juncea	Xanthorrhoea macronema	Hibbertia scandens	Zoysia macrantha

28

STRAND (<150 YEARS OLD)
OPEN GRASSLAND – SEDGELAND – HERBLAND

The Strand describes the beach and the low undulating sand dunes to 5 metres high immediately behind the beach above the high-water mark and located predominantly on the eastern side of the island. The two main plant communities found on the Strand are open grasslands on the newly formed dunes close to the ocean and those in the nearby depressions, or seepage areas (swales) which are dominated by sedges and herbs. These patches of herbs and sedges associated with the fresh water on the eastern beach are a feature of Fraser Island / K'gari, rarely seen on other nearby sand islands.

Carex pumila or strand sedge, colonises the newly deposited sand as the first step in the succession process. Due to its rhizomatous habit of sending out roots and shoots from the nodes, it covers the sand quickly and helps in its stabilisation. *Spinifex sericeus*, or beach spinifex, is a grass that grows up to 0.5 metres tall and is the dominant species on some exposed and recently formed sand. Often, it is found in pure stands quite a distance inland, notably close to Hook Point. The grasses *Eragrostis interrupta* and *Zoysia macrantha* are found here as well. In the drier regions surrounding the seepage areas, *Spinifex sericeu*s can also be found.

Further inland, large areas of the creeper *Ipomoea pes-caprae* and *Carpobrotus glaucescens* are seen with another plant with a purple bean like flower, the climbing herbaceous *Canavalia rosea*.

The creeper *Bacopa monnieri*, found in the moist areas or swales, often forms a mat which traps moving sand, helping to stabilize it by forming mounds about 0.5 metres in diameter.

Other species found in these moist areas include: herbs such as *Scaevola calendulacea, Triglochin striata, Zoysia macrantha, Lobelia anceps* and *Philydrum lanuginosum*. The deeper seepage areas further inland resemble small swamps (swales) and contain: *Fimbristylis nutans, Triglochin striata, Centella asiatica, Bacopa monnieri, Eleocharis caribaea, Eleocharis difformis* and *Eleocharis geniculate*. On the perimeter of these seepage areas, *Melastoma malabathricum*, a shrub with a distinctive bluish flower, and *Oenothera drummondii* grow along with *Nymphoides exiliflora, Eriocaulon scariosum* and *Digitaria* sp.

Figure 6 shows the relative location of some common plant species in a cross-section of a typical dune landform profile of the Strand, Fore Dune and Hind Dune on the east coast of Fraser Island / K'gari.

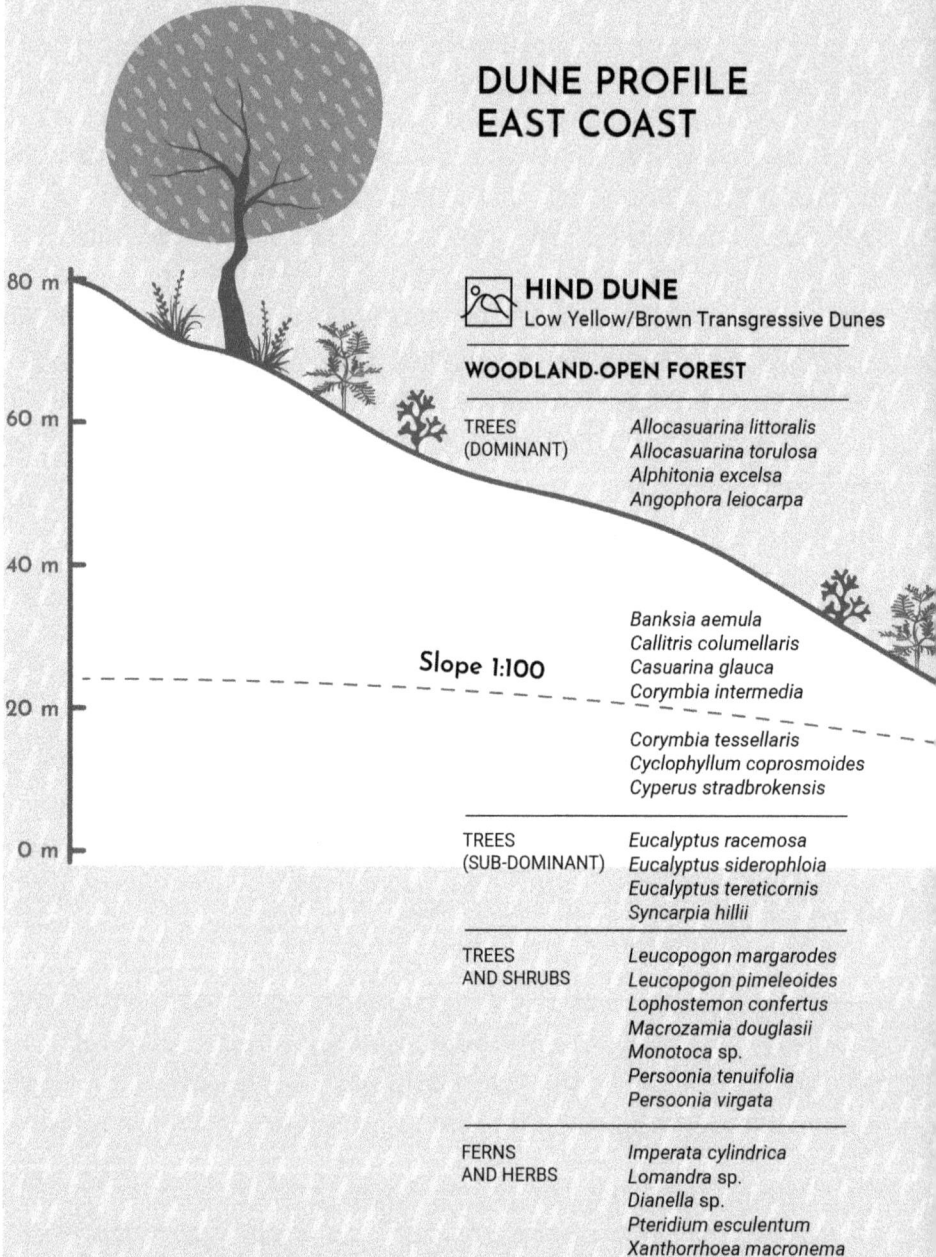

DUNE PROFILE
EAST COAST

80 m

HIND DUNE
Low Yellow/Brown Transgressive Dunes

WOODLAND-OPEN FOREST

TREES (DOMINANT)	*Allocasuarina littoralis*
	Allocasuarina torulosa
	Alphitonia excelsa
	Angophora leiocarpa

60 m

40 m

Banksia aemula
Callitris columellaris
Casuarina glauca
Corymbia intermedia

Slope 1:100

20 m

Corymbia tessellaris
Cyclophyllum coprosmoides
Cyperus stradbrokensis

0 m

TREES (SUB-DOMINANT)	*Eucalyptus racemosa*
	Eucalyptus siderophloia
	Eucalyptus tereticornis
	Syncarpia hillii

TREES AND SHRUBS	*Leucopogon margarodes*
	Leucopogon pimeleoides
	Lophostemon confertus
	Macrozamia douglasii
	Monotoca sp.
	Persoonia tenuifolia
	Persoonia virgata

FERNS AND HERBS	*Imperata cylindrica*
	Lomandra sp.
	Dianella sp.
	Pteridium esculentum
	Xanthorrhoea macronema

FIGURE 6: Typical cross-section of the Strand, Fore Dune and Hind Dune on the east coast of Fraser Island / K'gari showing common plant species.

FORE DUNE
Undulating Low Dunes

LOW WOODLAND-LOW-OPEN FOREST

TREES	Banksia integrifolia
	Casuarina equisetifolia var. Incana
	Pandanus tectorius
SHRUBS	Hibiscus diversifolius
	Lantana camara
HERBS	Carpobrotus glaucescens
	Centella asiatica
	Dianella caerulea
	Digitaria didactyla
	Eleocharis difformis

STRAND
Beach Fore Dunes

GRASSLAND -SEDGELAND-HERBLAND

SHRUBS	Melastoma malabathricum
HERBS	Bacopa monnieri
	Carex pumila
	Centella asiatica
	Eriocaulon scariosum
	Digitaria leucostachya
	Eleocharis caribaea
	Eleocharis ochrostachys
	Fimbristylis nutans
	Lobelia alata

SWALES

SWALES

CORAL SEA

	Eragrostis interrupta
	Ischaemum triticeum
	Nymphoides exiliflora
	Oenothera drummondii
	Scaevola calendulacea
	Zoysia macrantha
VINES	Hibbertia scandens

SWALES

HERBS	Bacopa monnieri
	Baumea rubiginosa
	Centella asiatica
	Cyperus polystachyos
AQUATIC HERBS	Triglochin procera
	Triglochin striata
	Philydrum lanuginosum

	Oenothera drummondii
	Nymphoides exiliflora
	Spinifex sericeus
	Zoysia macrantha
VINES	Ipomoea pes-caprae
AQUATIC HERBS	Philydrum lanuginosum

FORE DUNE (7,000 – 10,000 YEARS OLD)
SCRUBLAND – LOW WOODLAND – LOW OPEN FOREST

The Fore Dune includes dunes between 5 metres to 20 metres elevation and seepage areas or swales of varying sizes. These develop where freshwater seeps out from the higher dunes located further inland.

The area is rich in species with variable forms and habit. Directly behind the Strand, *Ipomoea pes caprae* still persists, along with *Zoysia* spp.*, Carex pumila, Oenothera* spp. and *Ischaemum triticeum. Sesuvium portulacastrum*, a herb with purple flowers, is seen on higher parts of the dune.

The swales contain the herbs *Cladium procerum, Ficinia nodosa, Triglochin procera* and *Baumea rubiginosa*, in the deeper water. Terrestrial herbs such as *Bacopa monnieri, Fimbristylis nutans, Utricularia biloba, Utricularia lateriflora, Triglochin striata* and shrubs such as *Hibiscus diversifolius* (swamp hibiscus) occupy the shallow regions.

On the western side of the swales, the dunes are often covered with *Hibbertia scandens*, a woody vine with a yellow flower. Along the western sides of the swales in the Fore Dune are found *Eragrostis interrupta, Oxalis corniculata*, the legume *Glycine tabacina* and small trees of the distinctive *Pandanus tectorius* (long leaved pandanus or screw pine) with its many branches, prop roots and yellow segmented fruits.

Pandanus tectorius is often found on the boundary with the Strand, usually in association with *Casuarina equisetifolia* var. *incana* (coastal she oak). She oak grows to 4 metres high and is seen in pure stands, easily recognised by its long pendulous green needle-like foliage. This is the species planted on the mined area which is seen from the beach and stretches from just north of Hook Point to the Dilli Village turnoff, just south of Second Creek.

Banksia integrifolia (coastal banksia) is a common tree which grows all over the Fore Dune. It has greenish-yellow flowers, grey bark and its leaves are green on the upper surface and lighter green underneath. Unusually, it has no serrations on the margins of the leaves, unlike many other banksias. It can be seen in various stages of development in woodland communities up to 10 metres tall in similar positions in the landscape to *Casuarina equisetifolia* var. *incana*. Shrubs are sparse, although shrubby forms of *Casuarina equisetifolia* var. *incana* and *Cupaniopsis anacardioides* occur. Ground cover species including: *Cyperus polystachyos, Dianella revoluta, Lobelia purpurascens, Melastoma malabathricum, Poranthera microphylla* and *Sphaeromorphaea australis* are common (Figure 6).

HIND DUNE (250,000 – 10,000 YEARS OLD)
WOODLAND – OPEN FOREST

The Hind Dune ranges in height from 20 to 80 metres elevation. They are covered in woodland-open forest, dominated by sclerophyll tree species with a xeromorphic (dry) shrubby understorey and a sparse ground layer of herbs and grasses.

These woodlands and forests are a mixture of low and medium height tree species, often dominated by *Angophora leiocarpa, Corymbia intermedia, Eucalyptus latisinensis, Eucalyptus pilularis, Eucalyptus racemosa* (scribbly gum), *Lophostemon confertus* and *Syncarpia hillii*. Other less common tree species include: *Callitris columellaris, Corymbia tessellaris, Eucalyptus latisinensis, Eucalyptus resinifera, Eucalyptus siderophloia, Eucalyptus tereticornis* and *Eucalyptus umbra*.

The species of small trees or shrubs found on ridges and in gullies in the banksia dominated woodlands include: *Acacia disparrima, Acacia flavescens, Acacia leiocalyx, Allocasuarina torulosa, Alphitonia excelsa, Banksia aemula, Banksia integrifolia, Boronia rivularis, Cupaniopsis anacardioides, Cyclophyllum coprosmoides, Hovea acutifolia, Jagera pseudorhus, Leptospermum trinervium, Leucopogon margarodes, Leucopogon parviflorus, Lophostemon confertus, Monotoca* sp., *Persoonia cornifolia, Persoonia stradbrokensis, Persoonia virgata, Petalostigma pubescens* and *Phebalium woombye*.

Common species in the ground stratum are: *Acacia suaveolens, Aotus ericoides, Astrotricha longifolia, Austromyrtus dulcis, Boronia rosmarinifolia, Caustis blakei, Caustis recurvata, Cyperus stradbrokensis, Dianella caerulea, Hibbertia scandens, Hovea longifolia, Hardenbergia violacea, Macrozamia douglasii, Pteridium esculentum, Smilax glyciphylla* and *Xanthorrhoea macronema*. The grasses seen here include: *Elionuris citreus* and *Themeda triandra*. Often, the ground layer in the gullies is dominated by *Imperata cylindrica* (blady grass) which is also a common invasive species that covers much of the fire-prone degraded lands in South-East Asia (Figure 6).

PHOTO 1
Common plants on the Strand and Fore Dune on the east coast of Fraser Island / K'gari.

35

PHOTO 2

Plant communities which occur in seepage areas (swales) on the eastern side of Fraser Island / K'gari are dominated by sedges and herbs.

PHOTO 3

Vegetation on the Fore Dune is often dominated by *Banksia integrifolia* up to 10 m tall.

PHOTO 4

Hind Dune vegetation is a mixture of low to medium height sclerophyll tree species of *Angophora leiocarpa, Corymbia intermedia* and *Eucalyptus racemosa.*

36

PHOTO 5

Open forests on the ridges and exposed sites on the High Dune.

PHOTO 6

Vegetation on the High Dune in open woodland on the western side of the island showing shrubs up to 2 m in height with a ground cover of between 30 and 50 %.

HIGH DUNE (500,000 – 120,000 YEARS OLD)
HIGHER DUNE – RIDGES

OPEN FOREST – TALL OPEN FOREST
This formation is dominated by the family Myrtaceae, with a foliage cover of between 30% and 70 % and tree heights varying between 10 and 30 metres+. The understorey consists of small trees and shrubs with some xeromorphic shrubs present.

The forests on these high ridges contain two main forest types: one dominated by *Eucalyptus pilularis* (blackbutt) and the other dominated by two tree genera, *Lophostemon confertus* (brush box) and *Syncarpia hillii* (satinay). Considered as a 'transition forest', it has a tendency toward that of a closed forest, with rainforest species in the understorey. The understorey in these open forests can either be sparse or dense and generally contains quite a range of rainforest tree species, shrubs and epiphytes.

The open and tall open forests on the ridges and more exposed sites are dominated by *Eucalyptus pilularis* (Photo 5). In the more sheltered regions, *Lophostemon confertus* and *Syncarpia hillii* dominate. These two species which dominate the satinay-brush box forests are usually greater than 30 metres in height. The *Syncarpia hillii* in this highly developed form is restricted to Fraser Island / K'gari. This forest type extends from Lake Bowarrady in the north in an almost continuous swathe to south of Fig Tree Lake and occurs on the deeper soils of the higher dunes.

Often, the understorey is sparse and is mostly vines and the shrub *Backhousia myrtifolia*, which is not common on the mainland. Other species found in these forests include: *Neolitsea dealbata*, *Notelaea longifolia* and *Syzygium oleosum*, the latter being easily recognised by its 1-2 cm diameter, round, purple fruits. Common vines include: *Callerya megasperma*, *Cissus* sp., *Flagellaria indica*, with its distinct tendrils, *Hoya australis*, *Ripogonum discolor* and *Smilax australis*, or barbed wire vine, named in reference to the presence of many barbs on the stem.

Ground species include: the common fern, *Blechnum cartilagineum*, the easily recognisable *Macrozamia douglasii*, which can form almost pure stands in some locations and the tufted herb *Lomandra laxa*.

The *Eucalyptus pilularis* (blackbutt) dominated forests cover over 14,000 ha and are found on the well-drained high ridges and the edges of the satinay-brush box forests. Blackbutt occurs at its most northern extent on Fraser Island / K'gari and grows in mosaic patches of almost even age, the result of natural or anthropogenic (people-started) fires, clearing or cyclonic activity. *Eucalyptus pilularis* is often associated with *Macrozamia douglasii*, which is a nitrogen fixing species and is a very conspicuous component in the understorey, not commonly seen outside this association.

Other tree species found as co-dominants or sub-dominants in other vegetation associations include: *Allocasuarina torulosa, Angophora leiocarpa,* scattered *Corymbia intermedia, Eucalyptus racemosa, Eucalyptus resinifera* and large *Eucalyptus microcorys* on the high transgressive dunes in the centre of the island.

The small trees and shrubs which dominate the understorey in the mid and lower stratum include: *Acacia flavescens, Acronychia imperforata, Alyxia ruscifolia, Backhousia myrtifolia, Banksia aemula, Boronia rosmarinifolia, Cryptocarya* spp., *Elaeocarpus reticulatus, Halfordia kendak, Jagera pseudorhus, Monotoca* sp., *Notelaea longifolia,* and *Polyscias elegans* along with saplings and coppices of *Lophostemon confertus* and *Syncarpia hillii*.

The ground layer in much of this forest contains: *Austromyrtus dulcis, Breynia oblongifolia, Caustis blakei, Dianella caerulea, Dodonaea triquetra, Lomandra longifolia, Macrozamia douglasii, Phebalium woombye, Themeda triandra* and *Xanthorrhoea macronema.* *Schizaea dichotoma* grows in protected areas, usually at the base of trees, while *Smilax australis, S. glyciphylla* and *Imperata cylindrica* are common in the more open areas.

HIGHER DUNES – LOWER SLOPES

FLATS
OPEN HEATH – LOW OPEN WOODLAND
This association contains shrubs up to 2 metres in height with a ground cover of between 30% and 50 %. *Eucalyptus racemosa* and *Banksia aemula* are the

dominant tree species which co-habit the dunes in this association, reaching a height of 5 metres (Photo 6). Heath species commonly found include: *Acacia suaveolens, Acacia ulicifolia, Aotus ericoides, Boronia falcifolia, Bossiaea ensata, Homoranthus virgatus, Leptospermum liversidgei, Leptospermum polygalofolium, Leptospermum semibaccatum, Ochrosperma lineare, Pimelea linifolia* and *Xanthorrhoea fulva*, as well as the parasite *Cassytha filiformis* entwined in the foliage.

Sedges found in the drainage lines include: *Baloskion tenuiculme, Baloskion tetraphyllum* and *Schoenus ornithopodioides*, while *Gahnia sieberiana* dominates the very moist regions with *Sporadanthus caudata* as a subdominant species.

SWAMPS/LAKES
SEDGELAND – WOODLAND

The perimeter of most lakes and swamps contains a narrow, 10 metre-wide strip of *Melaleuca quinquenervia* with *Lepironia articulata* and *Schoenus brevifolius* growing beneath. These species give way to *Ficinia nodosa* and *Lepidosperma longitudinale* close to the water's edge with *Lepironia articulata* in water up to 1 metre deep. Other species found in most of the lakes include: *Baumea articulata, Baumea rubiginosa* and *Baumea teretifolia* (Photo 7).

VALLEYS
CLOSED FOREST – TALL CLOSED FOREST

This forest type, colloquially termed 'rainforest', is confined mainly to the central part of Fraser Island / K'gari. It is well developed in the vicinity of Lake Bowarrady, Lake Allom, AB Lake, Bogimbah, Yidney Scrub and Wanggoolba and Eli Creeks. However, the most luxuriant development is around Wanggoolba Creek at Central Station. These closed forests cover over 10,000 hectares on the island and include vine forests with and without emergent *Araucaria cunninghamii*, tall *Syncarpia hillii* or *Lophostemon confertus*. In some areas, *Backhousia myrtifolia* grows in low vine forests with and without emergent *Araucaria cunninghamii*. Figure 2 provides the locations of these rainforest areas.

Pile Valley

The tallest stratum in this vegetation association ranges from 20 metres to 30+ metres in height and has a foliage cover of above 70%. At Central Station there is a dense patch of *Archontophoenix cunninghamiana* in an almost pure stand in the sheltered region at the headwaters of Wanggoolba Creek, close to Pile Valley. Palms are found in sheltered areas on the banks of other permanent streams, sometimes in association with *Syncarpia hillii, Syzygium luehmannii* and *S. oleosum* as shown in Figure 7.

Species commonly found in the closed forests include a large number of species found in the 'rainforests' on the mainland such as: *Agathis robusta, Elaeocarpus grandis, Euroshinus falcatus, Flindersia schottiana, Gmelina leichhardtii, Litsea australis, Lophostemon confertus, Pleioluma queenslandica, Syncarpia hillii, Syzygium oleosum, Schizomeria ovata*, with *Cinnamomum oliveri*, often seen in the upper stratum. Smaller trees and shrubs found in the middle and lower stratum include: *Alyxia ruscifolia, Backhousia myrtifolia, Eupomatia laurina, Mischocarpus pyriformis, Neolitsea dealbata, Rhodamnia acuminata, Schizomeria ovata, Syzygium luehmannii* and *Wilkiea macrophylla* along with numerous vines, ferns and orchids.

Species found near the edge of streams include: *Angiopteris evecta, Blechnum camfieldii, Dicksonia youngiae, Myrsine arenicola, Syzygium johnsonii, Tasmannia insipida* and *Todea barbara*. A couple of species peculiar to this forest type are the *Angiopteris evecta*, found on the banks of Wanggoolba Creek at Central Station (Photo 8) and *Macrozamia douglasii*, which normally does not grow under such a dense canopy.

Another peculiarity about tall closed forests on the island is that *Araucaria cunninghamii* (hoop pine) occurs naturally only in the north, past Boomerang Lakes, Lake Coomboo and Lake Bowarrady. The *Araucaria cunninghamii* plantations seen near the car park at Central Station were established using seedlings transported from the mainland and not from seed from the island's natural forests [29].

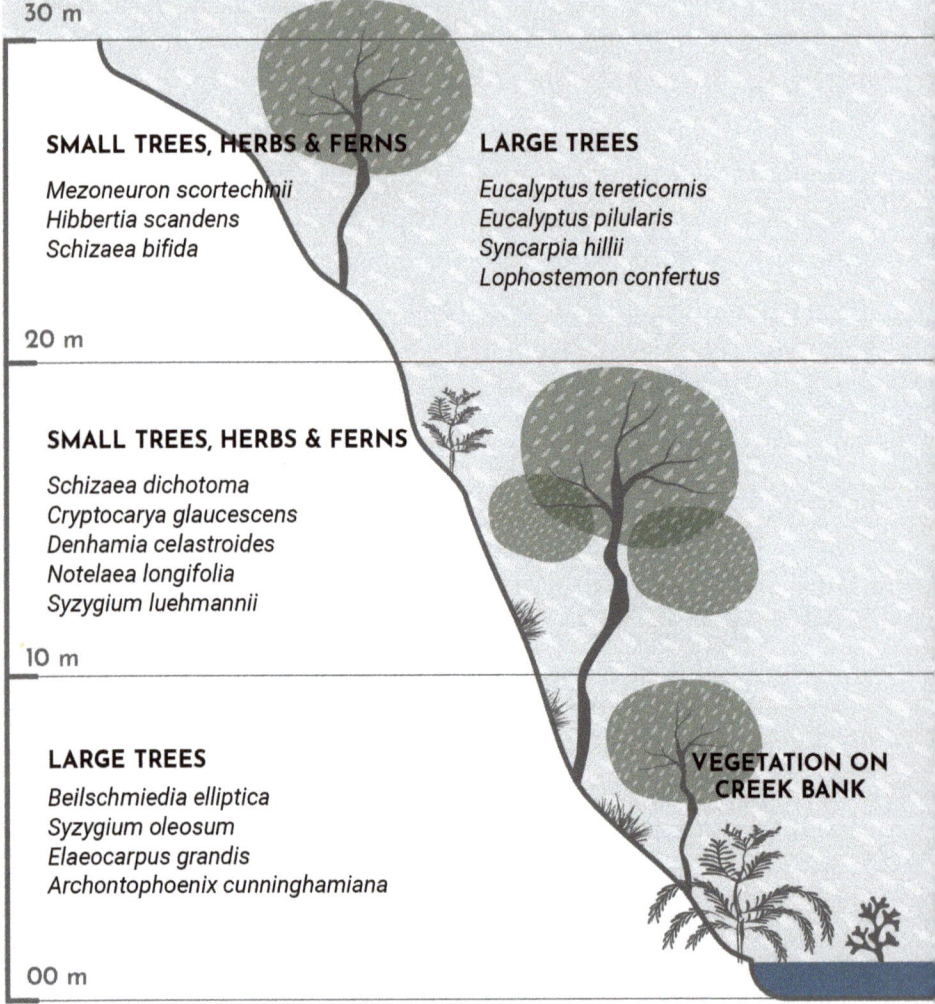

WANGGOOLBA CREEK-CENTRAL STATION TALL CLOSED-CLOSED FOREST

30 m

SMALL TREES, HERBS & FERNS

Mezoneuron scortechinii
Hibbertia scandens
Schizaea bifida

LARGE TREES

Eucalyptus tereticornis
Eucalyptus pilularis
Syncarpia hillii
Lophostemon confertus

20 m

SMALL TREES, HERBS & FERNS

Schizaea dichotoma
Cryptocarya glaucescens
Denhamia celastroides
Notelaea longifolia
Syzygium luehmannii

10 m

LARGE TREES

Beilschmiedia elliptica
Syzygium oleosum
Elaeocarpus grandis
Archontophoenix cunninghamiana

VEGETATION ON CREEK BANK

00 m

FIGURE 7: Cross section of Wanggoolba Creek at Central Station.

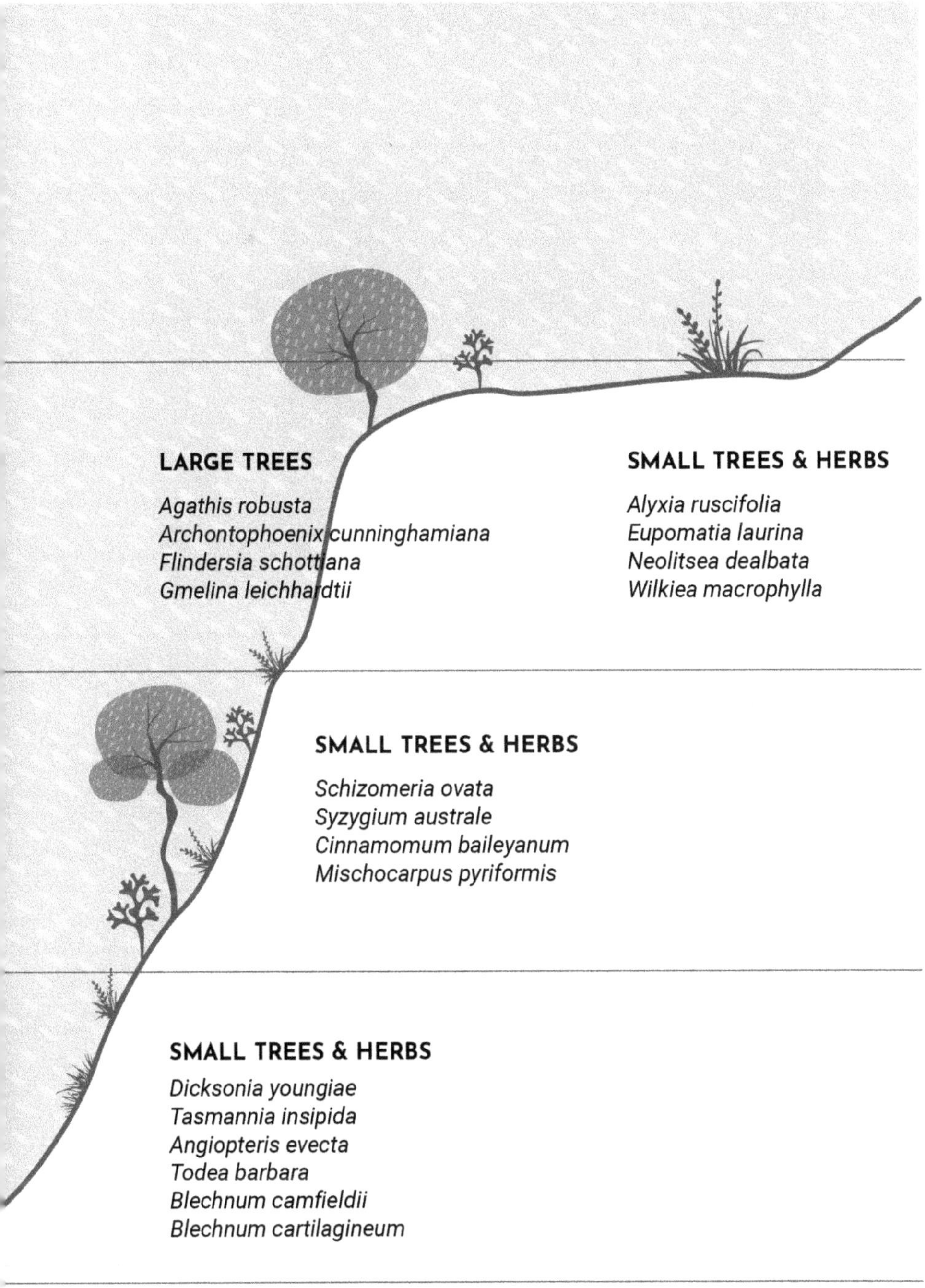

LARGE TREES

Agathis robusta
Archontophoenix cunninghamiana
Flindersia schottiana
Gmelina leichhardtii

SMALL TREES & HERBS

Alyxia ruscifolia
Eupomatia laurina
Neolitsea dealbata
Wilkiea macrophylla

SMALL TREES & HERBS

Schizomeria ovata
Syzygium australe
Cinnamomum baileyanum
Mischocarpus pyriformis

SMALL TREES & HERBS

Dicksonia youngiae
Tasmannia insipida
Angiopteris evecta
Todea barbara
Blechnum camfieldii
Blechnum cartilagineum

PHOTO 7

Lake Benaroon is typical of the numerous lakes found on the High Dune.

PHOTO 8

Wanggoolba Creek and surrounding vegetation.

LOWER DUNES – RIDGES

WOODLAND – OPEN FOREST

This vegetation association, on the lower dune systems of the High Dune, is widespread on the western side of the island, which contains most of the older sands. This vegetation association is common on the flats, low rises and hills, and contains fewer species than comparable areas on the mainland. Fire plays a major role here, with the species richness seen to be changing with the increase in fire frequency. There is a greater percentage of xerophytic species in the understorey than on the ridges of the High Dune. The tree foliage cover in this community is between 10% and 30% with the heights of the tallest individuals ranging from 10 metres to 30 metres.

The dominant and sometimes emergent tree species include: *Angophora leiocarpa, Callitris columellaris, Corymbia gummifera, Corymbia intermedia, Eucalyptus latisinensis* and *Eucalyptus racemosa*. Other less dominant species include: *Allocasuarina torulosa, Banksia aemula, Melaleuca quinquenervia* and saplings of *Syncarpia hillii.*

The shrub layer consists of *Monotoca* sp. in the south of the island, while *Monotoca scoparia* is found mainly in the northern part of Fraser Island / K'gari. *Acacia* spp., *Leptospermum liversidgei, Leucopogon margarodes, Persoonia virgata* and *Phebalium woombye* are present in areas where fire is less prevalent or subjected to less disturbance.

The ground stratum is sparse, but *Themeda triandra* dominates in many areas. Other species include: *Digitaria* sp., *Entolasia stricta* and the fern *Pteridium esculentum.*

LOWER DUNES – LOWER SLOPES

FLATS
CLOSED HEATH – OPEN SCRUB

Species in these vegetation formations consist of evergreen shrubs and low eucalypt/banksia in mallee form. The density ranges from 70 % to 100 % in the closed heaths to 30% to 70% in the eucalypt/banksia communities on the drier sites.

Grasses are rare, but annual herbs can be readily seen after the wet season, following fire. Sedges abound in many moist areas. These formations usually occur on peats or humic podzols which are damp for much of the year. The larger tree species which dominate the drier areas include: *Acacia disparrima*, *Banksia aemula* and *Eucalyptus latisinensis*, while *Leptospermum polygalifolium* is found in the lower stratum.

The canopy height of the heath varies from 1 to 2 metres, with *Acacia suaveolens*, *Acacia ulicifolia*, *Banksia robur*, *Dillwynia floribunda*, *Leptospermum liversidgei* and *Leptospermum polygalifolium* being the common species found here.

The ground stratum contains herbs such as *Blandfordia grandiflora* (Photo 9) and *Stylidium ornatum*; both of these are particularly evident following fire. The Restionaceae and Cyperaceae families are present in large numbers and species to be found include: *Baloskion pallens*, *Caustis recurvata*, *Gahnia sieberiana* and *Schoenus* spp.

PHOTO 9

The ground orchid *Blandfordia grandiflora* or Christmas Bell is a common sight in the wallum with a regular burning regime. Photo: Jerry Vanclay

VALLEYS
LOW WOODLAND – LOW OPEN FOREST
The dune areas surrounding the creeks on the western fringes fall into this category. The tree species which dominate include: *Angophora leiocarpa, Eucalyptus tereticornis, Lophostemon suaveolens* and *Melaleuca quinquenervia.*

The understorey includes some of the heath species and, in the wetter areas, *Baloskion tetraphyllum, Gahnia sieberiana*, and members of the Cyperaceae family dominate.

LITTORAL FLATS

SEDGELAND – GRASSLAND – HERBLAND – WOODLAND – LOW OPEN FOREST
The many species of the mangrove forest dominate this community in the low/ open forest in the intertidal zone. *Avicennia marina* (Photo 10) is the dominant mangrove and grows to 9 metres in height. *Ceriops tagal, Osbornia octodonta* and *Rhizophora stylosa* grow in the vicinity of the *Avicennia marina* with *Aegiceras corniculatum* and *Bruguiera gymnorhiza* growing on the landward side of these species. Further inland, *Excoecaria agallocha* grows to 3 metres in height where *Lumnitzera racemosa* is found.

Beneath the mangroves, herbs such as *Suaeda arbusculoides* and *Tecticornia halocnemoides* are evident. *Tecticornia indica* subsp. *leiostachya* develop in areas which are inundated at high tide and dry out at low tide.
The salt marsh and clay pans (salt flats) which lie between the High Dune and the mangroves contain semi-freshwater drainage lines. These areas are dominated by rushes and sedges including: *Baumea* spp., *Cyperus* spp., *Ficinia nodosa, Fimbristylis ferruginea, Fimbristylis polytrichoides, Juncus kraussii* and *Triglochin striata. Sporobolus virginicus* is found near the margins of these areas, while *Sesuvium portulacastrum* is found where there is a greater percentage of sand.

There is a transition area between the salt marsh and the High Dune which is dominated by *Casuarina glauca* and *Melaleuca quinquenervia* in various shapes and heights. Further inland from the margin dominated by *Casuarina glauca*, species such as *Acacia* spp., *Banksia aemula, Corymbia intermedia* and *Eucalyptus tereticornis* occur in woodland formations. The creeper *Cissus hypoglauca* is found in the ground stratum while *Passiflora pallida*, a corky stemmed vine, is prevalent over much of the area and on the stems of the trees and shrubs. A cross-section of the communities in the Littoral Flats on the west coast is shown in Figure 8.

FIGURE 8: Littoral Flats communities on the west coast of Fraser Island / K'gari.

LITTORAL FLATS WEST COAST

HIGH DUNE
LOW OPEN FOREST-WOODLAND

Eucalyptus intermedia
Eucalyptus tereticornis
Acacia leiocalyx
Tristania suaveolons
Melaleuca quinquenervia
Casuarina glauca
Dianella sp.
Eriochloa procera
Ischnostemma carnosum
Myoporum ellipticum
Hibiscus tillaceus
Vernonia cinerea
Passiflora pallida
Lomandra longifolia
Sporobolus virginicus

GREAT
SANDY
STRAIT

LITTORAL COMMUNITIES

SALT MARSH
GRASSLAND-HERBLAND

Fimbristylis ferruginea
Fimbristiylis polytrichoides
Juncus kraussi
Arthrocnemum leiostachyum
Arthrocnemum halocnemoides
Eragrotis interrupta
Baumea juncea
Limonium australe
Axonopus conprenssus

MANGROVE COMMUNITY
LOW/OPEN FOREST

Sporobolus diandra
Sporobolus virginicus
Suaeda australis
Suaeda harbusculoides
Sesuvium portulacastrum
Ranalina sp.
Teloschistes sp.
Aegialitis annulata
Ceriops tagal
Aegiceras corniculatum
Avicennia marina
Excoecaria agallocha
Lumnitzera racemosa
Osbornea octodonta
Rhizophona stylosa
Ameyema sp.

50

PHOTO 10

Littoral Flats communities on the west coast. The two photos taken in 1980 and again from a similar location in 2015 show the changes to the intertidal zone. *Avicennia marina* is the dominant mangrove in the transition area on the left-hand side of the photographs and is found in the area between the salt marsh and the dunes. This area is dominated by *Casuarina glauca* and *Melaleuca quinquenervia* at various stages of development.

FOREST BIOMASS PRODUCTIVITY AND NUTRIENT STATUS

FOREST BIOMASS

An interesting question when visiting Pile Valley, with its towering *Syncarpia hillii* trees, or the large *Eucalyptus pilularis* forests near Central Station might be: "How can such huge trees grow and thrive on nutritionally poor white siliceous sands?"

The height and diameter of the trees in the forests on the high young dunes on the eastern side of the island which have a shallow depth to the B horizon (yellow /brown sand), are larger than the trees on the high older dunes located on the western side of the island, which have a deeper depth to the B horizon, and have been leeched heavily of nutrients. However, these tall forests are not maintained by the nutrient content of the soils, which is very poor. They are nourished by the cycling of nutrients deposited by the wind and rain and distributed between the various ecosystem components and mycorrhizal associations. Thus, balancing the inputs and outputs of nutrients available to the small trees, understorey plants and forest litter.

Commercial logging practices, silvicultural treatments, burning and cyclones, have all impacted on the nutrient capital and productivity of the island's forests. The impact of some of these disturbances was quantified by assessing biomass and nutrient stocks present in the total plant material (both above and below ground), as well measuring the soil nutrient content at different stages in the development of the blackbutt forests.

Three growth stages of *Eucalyptus pilularis* forests were sampled to determine the biomass based on: a sapling dominated site, a pole site and a mature/over-mature stage forest. The total biomass (expressed as oven dry weight) of the three stages of the blackbutt dominated forests are: sapling 413 t/ha, pole 639 t/ha and over-mature 1,996 t/ha. The component weights of the three forests on Fraser Island / K'gari are shown in Figure 9. Note that the rate at which the sapling and pole stage forest accumulates biomass (nett primary production), is greater than the mature forest, even though the biomass is less in these two younger forests [33].

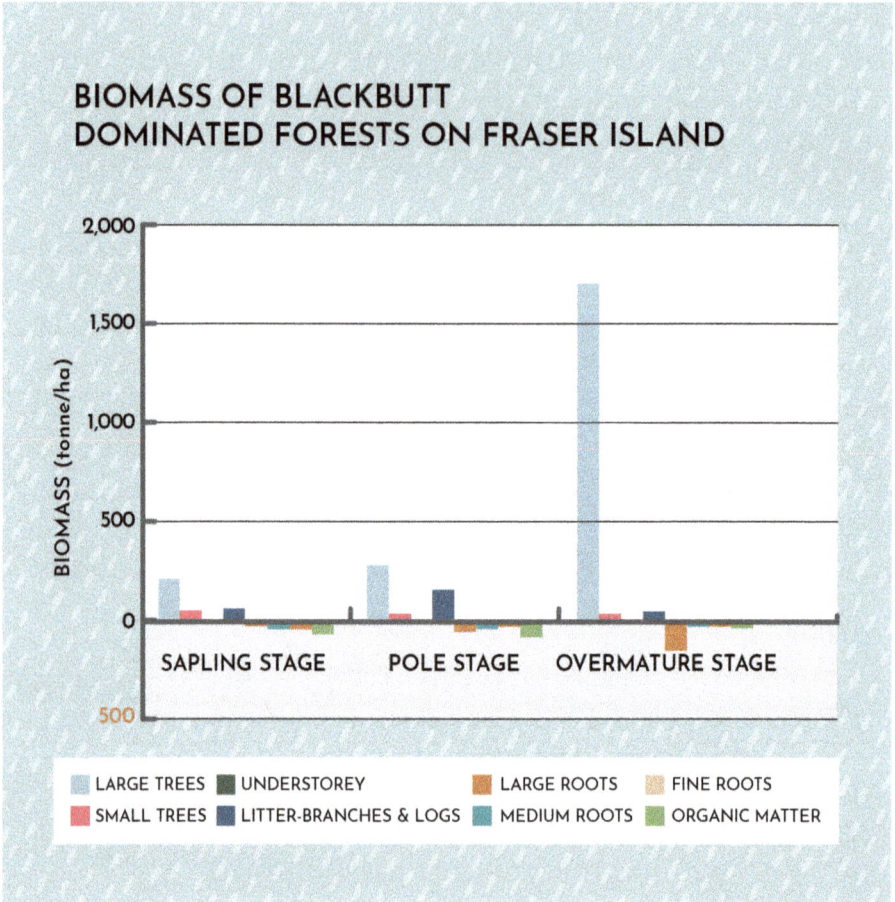

BIOMASS OF BLACKBUTT DOMINATED FORESTS ON FRASER ISLAND

LARGE TREES | UNDERSTOREY | LARGE ROOTS | FINE ROOTS
SMALL TREES | LITTER-BRANCHES & LOGS | MEDIUM ROOTS | ORGANIC MATTER

FIGURE 9: Estimated biomass of site three stages of growth of *Eucalyptus pilularis* dominated forests on Fraser Island / K'gari (tonne/ha).

SELF GUIDED VEGETATION DISCOVERY TOUR

Ten sites are suggested for self-guided driving and walking tours. These should illustrate the diversity and uniqueness of the plant communities on this World Heritage Listed island.

The map in Figure 10 shows the access routes to the sites which are numbered sequentially starting from Dilli Village and ending at the lookout at Lake Wabby.

The condition of the roads, which are sandy tracks, is dependent on the weather and can make driving times between sites variable, depending on the condition of the sand. The tracks are best driven after rain when the sand is moist.

Allow at least one hour at each site to explore the area, although some locations, such as Central Station, may take three hours.

Based on the suggested times for each site, the full tour could take up to two days by 4WD, with an overnight camping stop, either at Central Station or at Eurong township (a 20 minute detour to the beach, for hotel accommodation or camping and a general store).

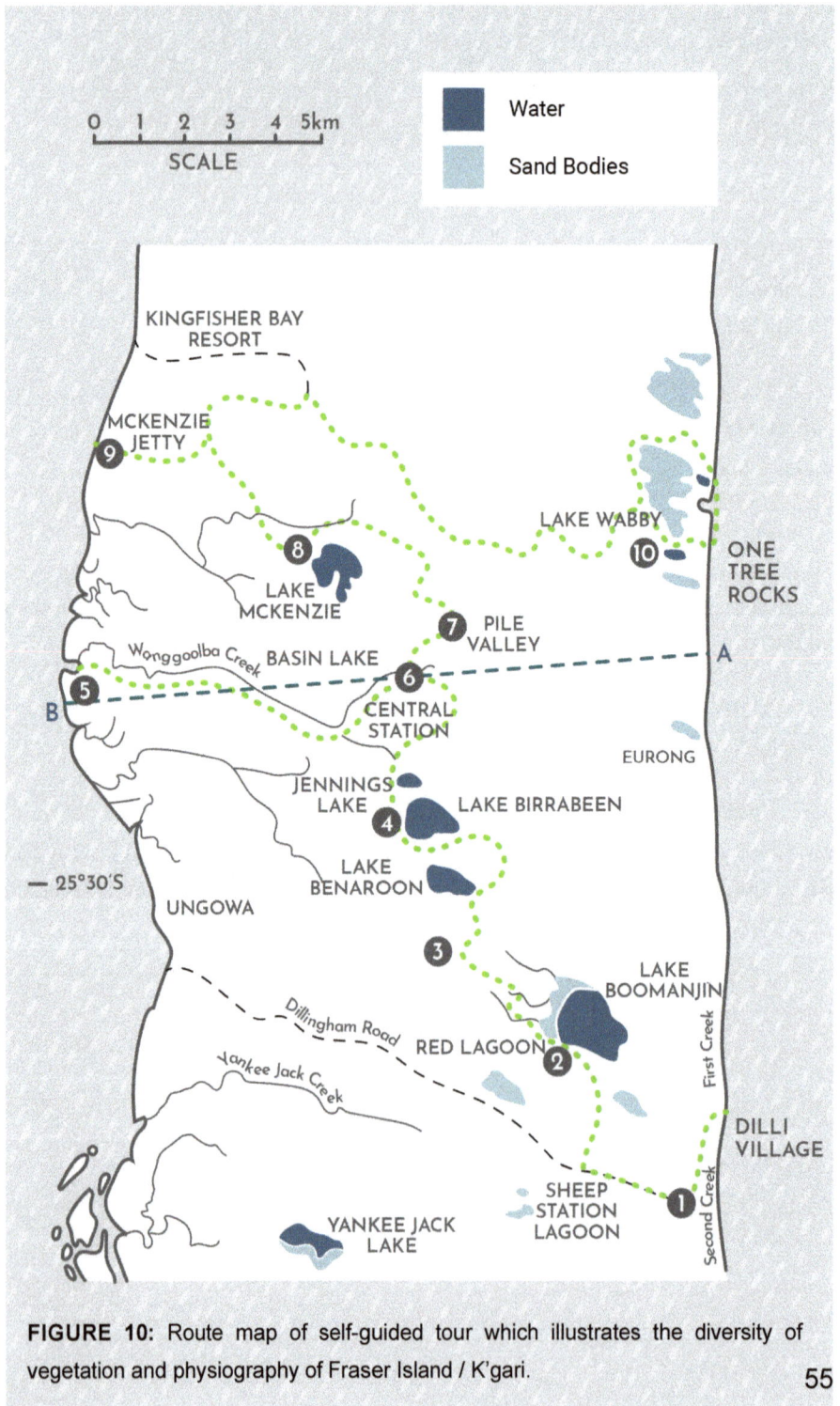

FIGURE 10: Route map of self-guided tour which illustrates the diversity of vegetation and physiography of Fraser Island / K'gari.

1. The tour commences on the east coast at the track leading off the beach to Dilli Village. (This is the University of the Sunshine Coast, Research and Learning Centre and camping ground.)
2. Proceed on the track towards the rehabilitated sand mining area, to the intersection with Dillingham Road, just south of Dilli Village.
3. Dillingham Road then continues across the island to Deep Creek on the west coast.
4. The tour sites are located on the main track to Lake Boomanjin, then Birrabeen Lake, the mouth of Wanggoolba Creek, Central Station and Pile Valley.
5. After Pile Valley the track turns north towards Lake McKenzie (*Lake Boorangoora*) and then west to the coast and McKenzie Jetty.
6. From there it leads back towards the east coast via Lake Wabby lookout.

SITE 1. REHABILITATED MINED AREA

Located on the northern end of the rehabilitated sand mining area, it is reached by turning south on the track which intersects Dillingham Road from Dilli Village. This was the Dillingham Mining camp for its workers on the island's sand-mining operation. Now it is managed by the University of the Sunshine Coast as a research and teaching facility.

The site provides a contrast between sand mined areas (revegetated in 1974/5), on the east side of the track, where there are stands of tall *Eucalyptus pilularis* and the natural, unmined woodland dominated by *Eucalyptus racemosa* (scribbly gum) on the western side of the track.

Parts of Fraser Island / K'gari and other areas of large coastal sand deposits in eastern Australia, were mined from the 1930s for minerals containing titanium dioxide, principally ilmenite and rutile. Exploratory leases for sand mining were granted in 1950, over a narrow strip of the east coast on Fraser Island / K'gari, covering 254 ha and expanded in the mid-1970s to cover more than 12,000 ha [34].

Mining commenced in 1971 and by 1976 covered an area of 233 ha along a narrow strip of land on the beach and fore dunes stretching from Dilli Village to Hook Point on the southern end of the island. Another area of 150 ha, which extended up to 1.5 to 2 km inland and up to 50-60 metres elevation, located southwest of Dilli Village, was mined by DM Minerals in 1975 and 1976. Sand mining ceased on the island in December 1976 after the Commonwealth Government stopped issuing export licences for the minerals produced [35].

The original vegetation on the mined area consisted of a mixture of sclerophyll species growing in woodland and open-forest with a height from 16 to 18 metres. Dominant tree species were: *Angophora leiocarpa, Corymbia intermedia, Corymbia tessellaris, Eucalyptus racemosa, Eucalyptus siderophloia* and *Lophostemon confertus* [36].

Small trees of *Acacia flavescens, Acacia leiocalyx, Allocasuarina littoralis, Banksia aemula, Banksia integrifolia, Casuarina equisetifolia* var. *incana,* and *Monotoca* sp. were present. Shrub and ground cover species included the conspicuous *Caustis blakei* [36].

The original vegetation was cleared prior to mining using a mulching machine (tritter), which cut and collected the forest understorey and stored it offsite. The land was then machine cleared and the soil was stripped to a depth of approximately 25-30 cm and stockpiled. The area was mined and the heavy minerals extracted. Following mining, the sand was replaced and contoured to the original topography. The topsoil, which had been stored for approximately three months during the mining process, was spread over the mined site to a depth of 25 cm. The mulching material collected from the areas prior to mining was spread uniformly over the mined areas at 18-22 tonnes dry weight per hectare. This application of mulch helped prevent wind erosion of the exposed sand and provided a cover to enhance planted and natural regeneration.

The Queensland Department of Forestry undertook a monitoring program and research including fertiliser and species trials on the rehabilitated areas [37]. The species planted in the trials by the Queensland Department of Forestry included: *Allocasuarina littoralis, Angophora leiocarpa, Banksia aemula, Banksia integrifolia, Corymbia intermedia, Eucalyptus pilularis, Eucalyptus racemosa, Lophostemon confertus, Melaleuca quinquenervia* and *Syncarpia hillii.*

In addition to the species planted, the species listed in Table 5 established themselves in some of the mined areas. The species in this list are representative of early successional stages of the development of the vegetation but are now less common [37].

SPECIES NAMES	
Acacia disparrima	Acacia flavescens
Acacia leiocalyx	Acacia suaveolens
Allocasuarina littoralis	Allocasuarina torulosa
Aristida benthami	Astrotricha longifolia
Banksia aemula	Bossiaea brownii
Bossiaea heterophylla	Brachyloma daphnoides
Carpobrotus glaucescens	Caustis blakei
Crassocephalum crepidioides	Cynodon dactylon
Cyperus cyperoides	Cyperus stradbrokensis
Dianella caerulea	Entolasia marginata
Eragrostis spartinoides	Eriachne pallescens
Eustrephus latifolius	Glycine clandestina
Glycine tomentella	Gompholobium pinnatum
Gompholobium virgatum	Goodenia rotundifolia
Hibbertia linearis	Hibbertia vestita
Homoranthus virgatus	Imperata cylindrica
Jacksonia scoparia	Lepidosperma laterale
Leucopogon leptospermoides	Leucopogon margarodes
Lomandra confertifolia	Macrozamia douglasii
Monotoca sp.	Paspalidium constrictum
Patersonia glabrata	Persoonia virgata
Phebalium woombye	Pimelea linifolia
Platysace lanceolata	Platysace linearifolia
Pomax umbellata	Poranthera microphylla
Pteridium esculentum	Pultenaea villosa
Smilax australis	Styphelia viridis

TABLE 5: Species known to have established on the mined area, in addition to those planted.

SITE 2. LAKE BOOMANJIN

Lake Boomanjin covers an area of about 200 ha and is the largest perched sand dune lake in the world.

OPEN-FOREST

The forests surrounding the lake at the camp/picnic site are dominated by *Eucalyptus pilularis* (blackbutt) which grows to between 20 and 25 metres high. It dominates the tall open-forest on the central ridges on the island [38]. Blackbutt is recognised by the stringy bark at the base of the trunk and smooth bark at the top in the crown. The bark at its base is often blackened by fire. The blackbutt dominated forests cover 10% of the island and make up a large part of the floristic component [39]. The forest consists of groups of mainly even-aged trees which have resulted from natural or artificial disturbances in the past. Blackbutt requires major site disturbance to enable successful establishment of the seedlings. Natural disturbances result from fire or cyclonic winds breaking up the forest and from dead and over-mature trees falling and creating gaps in the canopy. Often these gaps receive sufficient light to enable prolific seedling regeneration. Smaller trees of *Syncarpia hillii* are also present.

Shrubs, 3 to 4 metres high, of the following species are present in the understorey: *Banksia aemula, Dodonaea triquetra,*

Leptospermum polygalifolium, Leucopogon margarodes, Monotoca sp., *Phebalium woombye* and *Ricinocarpos pinifolius.*

Ground layer species, 1 to 2 metres high, include: *Boronia rosmarinifolia, Caustis blakei, Cassytha pubescens, Lomandra laxa, Platysace lanceolata, Pteridium esculentum, Schizaea bifida* and *Xanthorrhoea macronema.*

LAKE EDGE

The edge of Lake Boomanjin is surrounded in places by open-heath vegetation. Species of interest include: the *Drosera binata* (fork sundew) and *D. spatulata* (the spoon leaved sundew), which have red leaves covered with droplets of clear sticky liquid and are easily seen.

Other species include: *Empodisma minus* and *Selaginella uliginosa* (swamp selaginella). Sedges in the lagoon include: *Baumea articulata, Baumea rubiginusa, Baumea teretifolia* and *Lepironia articulata.*

The lake edge is sufficiently steep to exhibit, over a short distance, a gradient dominated by species from the families Cyperaceae and Restionaceae. Species groupings along the gradient are clearly distinguishable. The relative importance values associated with the composition of species, along a gradient of increasing elevation and increasing distance from the free waters' edge is shown in Figure 11 a and b.

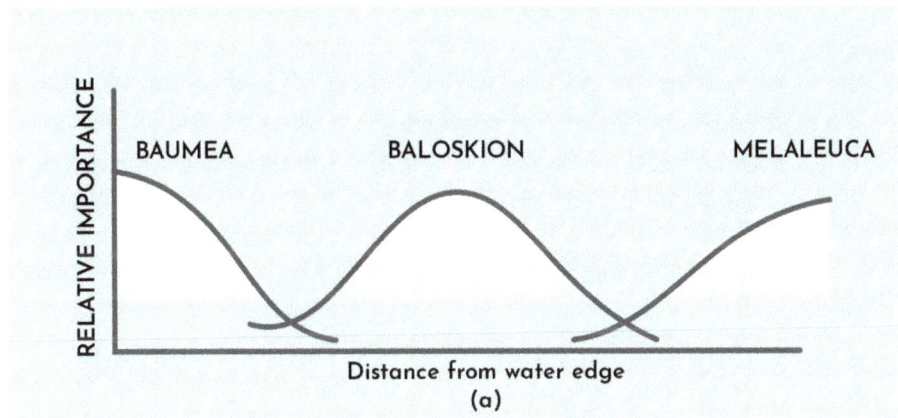

Distance from water edge
(a)

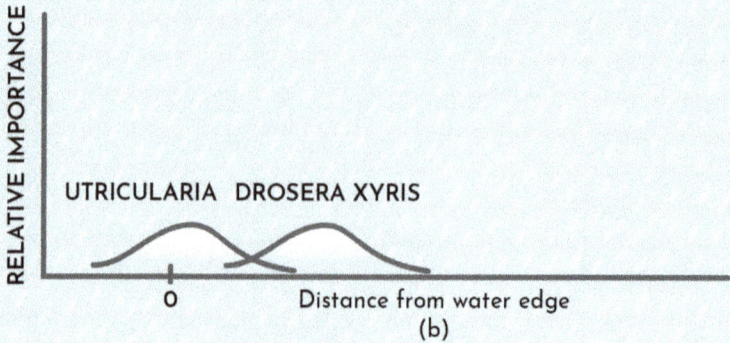

FIGURE 11: Species compositional gradient in many lakes on Fraser Island / K'gari.

a. Sequence of perennial species (*Baumea, Baloskion* and *Schoenus* spp.). This sequence grades into an upland *Melaleuca quinquenervia* woodland community.

b. Importance of *Drosera spatulata, Utricularia lateriflora* and *Xyris juncea* relative to water level.

The position of other species (*Drosera, Utricularia* and *Xyris*) is seen along a species gradient which at any one time is related to the prevailing water level. Additionally, *Lepironia articulata* is common in some of the shallow water areas, but also it extends out into the deepest parts of the lake.

SITE 3. WALLUM FORMATION

The land here is of low relief and forms part of the old lakebed of Lake Boomanjin. Formerly, the water level in the lake was higher and more expansive, but changes in coastline alignment, with sea level fluctuations, have led to water-table level changes.

Species commonly found in the wallum are listed in Table 6. Zonation of the species and species associations broadly corresponds to differences in topography and water-table depth.

The open-heath wallum communities found here are usually less than 2 metres high. The species composition of most wallum heaths found throughout south-eastern Queensland varies considerably from one site to another. However, the family composition varies less. Species of the families Restionaceae and Cyperaceae usually dominate the ground layer and shrub species of the Eriaceae, Fabaceae, Myrtaceae and Proteaceae families are common.

On slightly higher ground, the heath forms a ground-layer understorey with *Banksia aemula* open-scrub (small trees of 3 to 4 metres). Other species present in the open heath include: *Gompholobium pinnatum* and *Leptospermum semibaccatum*. The heath understorey continues into the 6 meters tall *Eucalyptus racemosa* dominated low woodland located on higher ground.

SEDGES	
CYPERACEAE	*Baumea rubiginusa, Gahnia sieberiana, Schoenus brevifolius*
RESTIONACEAE	*Sporadanthus caudata*

HEATH SPECIES	
CUNONIACEAE	*Bauera capitata*
CYPERACEAE	*Caustis recurvata, Gahnia sieberiana, Lepidosperma laterale, Schoenus ornithopodioides*
ERICACEAE	*Epacris pulchella, Leucopogon margarodes, Styphelia viridis*
EUPHORBIACEAE	*Ricinocarpos pinifolius*
FABACEAE	*Mirbelia rubiifolia*
HAEMODORACEAE	*Haemodorum tenuifolium*
LAURACEAE	*Cassytha filiformis, Cassytha pubescens*
LAXMANNIACEAE	*Laxmannia gracilis*
MYRTACEAE	*Baeckea frutescens, Leptospermum semibaccatum*
OLACACEAE	*Olax retusa*
PROTEACEAE	*Banksia robur, Conospermum taxifolium, Persoonia virgata, Petrophile shirleyae, Strangea linearis*
RESTIONACEAE	*Sporadanthus interruptus*
RUTACEAE	*Boronia falcifolia, Phebalium woombye*
SANTALACEAE	*Choretrum candollei*
STYLIDACEAE	*Stylidium ornatum*
THYMELAEACEAE	*Pimelea linifolia*
XANTHORRHOEACEAE	*Xanthorrhoea fulva*

BANKSIA AEMULA FORMATION	
FABACEAE	*Gompholobium pinnatum*
MYRTACEAE	*Leptospermum polygalifolium*

TABLE 6: Species of wallum communities north-west of Lake Boomanjin.

SITE 4. LAKE BIRRABEEN

Eucalyptus racemosa is the dominant tree species seen between the carpark and Lake Birrabeen. Other species present, particularly along the walking tracks leading to the lake, include two prominent Acacias. *Acacia suaveolens* which is a slender shrub with conspicuous angular branchlets with roundish white flowers and blue-black flat seed pods. *Acacia ulicifolia*, is a low shrub to 0.5 metres, with stiff erect hairs which gives it the common name of prickly moses.

Other species include: *Aotus ericoides, Aotus lanigera, Banksia aemula, Caustis blakei* and *Caustis recurvata*. The latter two species are from the family Cyperaceae and are perennial with erect cylindrical smooth stems containing many nodes. *Cassytha filiformis* is a parasite seen covering the low shrubs of *Chloanthes parviflora, Coleocarya gracilis, Laxmannia gracilis, Phebalium woombye* and *Pimelea linifolia*.

SITE 5. WANGGOOLBA CREEK MANGROVES

Eight species of mangroves, along with other species occurring at the mouth of Wanggoolba Creek, are listed in Table 7. A mixed species mangrove community is seen adjacent to the mouth of the creek and, to the south, away from the creek, the mangroves are dominated by *Ceriops tagal* var. *australis*. A decrease in the height of these communities is associated with higher ground, with less frequent inundations of sea water. Further inland and on higher ground, a marsh community dominated by *Sporobolus virginicus* occurs (abrupt changes to the topography may lead to the absence of this zone in some locations). *Tecticornia* sp. and *Suaeda* sp. can be seen in this higher tidal area.

LOWER TIDAL	
MANGROVES:	*Aegialitis annulata, Avicennia marina, Aegiceras corniculatum, Lumnitzera racemosa, Excoecaria agallocha, Osbornia octodonta, Ceriops tagal var. australis, Rhizophora stylosa*
FORBS:	*Tecticornia indica, Tecticornia halocnemoides, Suaeda australis, Suaeda arbusculoides*
MISTLETOE:	*Amyema mackayense*
HIGHER TIDAL	
TREES:	*Casuarina glauca*
TREES/SHRUBS:	*Hibiscus tiliaceus, Myoporum acuminatum*
GRASS:	*Sporobolus virginicus*
FORBS:	*Fimbristylis ferruginea, Fimbristylis polytrichoides, Juncus kraussii, Limonium solanderi, Sesuvium portulacastrum*

TABLE 7: Intertidal species occurring at the mouth of Wanggoolba Creek.

The transition between the tidal and supra-tidal land is clearly marked by the occurrence of non-mangrove sclerophyll trees on the landward side, as shown in Table 8. A fringe of *Casuarina glauca* is common in this area where the land is slightly higher and *Lophostemon suaveolens* and *Melaleuca quinquenervia* can also be seen.

The change in ground species is less distinct as a mixture of species occur. Some of the shrubs and ground layer species that occur near the edge of the supra-tidal zone near the mouth of Wanggoolba Creek are listed in Table 8.

TREE SPECIES
Casuarina glauca, Corymbia intermedia, Eucalyptus tereticornis, Lophostemon suaveolens, Melaleuca quinquenervia

SHRUB AND GROUND LAYER SPECIES
Acacia leiocalyx (shrub), *Baumea juncea, Dianella* spp., *Eriochloa procera, Lomandra longifolia, Passiflora pallida, Sporobolus virginicus*

TABLE 8: Tree, shrub and ground layer species near the edge of the supra-tidal zone.

SITE 6. CENTRAL STATION

Central Station was first established in 1920 by the Queensland Forest Service. The central part of the island was declared a forestry reserve in 1908 and the whole of the island declared State Forest by 1925. Central Station became the centre for forest management, with numerous reminders such as the Forestry Office and Workshop still present today. Harvesting of the blackbutt forests and other silvicultural activities ceased in December 1991 when the island was gazetted as a National Park. It obtained World Heritage Listing in 1992.

Listed in Table 9 are plant species seen at Central Station, between the old Forestry Department Office and west to the hoop pine plantation area, and along the Wanggoolba Creek board walk to the exit/entrance at the eastern end of Central Station.

AREA OPPOSITE INFORMATION CENTRE	
SAPLINGS TREES:	*Ficus obliqua, Archontophoenix cunninghamiana, Endiandra discolor, Jagera pseudorhus, Eucalyptus latisinensis Eucalyptus tereticornis, Syncarpia hillii*
VINES:	*Cissus hypoglauca, Geitonoplesium cymosum, Hibbertia scandens, Stephania japonica, Mezoneuron scortechinii*
EPIPHYTES/FERNS:	*Platycerium bifurcatum, Platycerium superbum, Ophioglossum pendulum*
ORCHIDS	*Dockrillia linguiformis, Oberonia palmicola*
GROUND COVER:	
FERNS:	*Nephrolepis cordifolia*
OTHER:	*Commelina diffusa, Macrozamia douglasii*
ADJACENT TO EUCALYPTUS GRANDIS STAND (PLANTED IN 1950)	
SAPLINGS/ TREES:	*Agathis robusta, Elaeocarpus eumundi, Elaeocarpus obovatus, Flindersia bennettii, Gmelina leichhardtii, Halfordia kendak, Litsea australis, Trochocarpa laurina*
PICNIC AREA AT CENTRAL STATION	
TREES:	*Araucaria bidwillii* (planted), *Araucaria cunninghamii* (plantation), *Grevillea robusta, Podocarpus elatus, Schizomeria ovata*
TRACK TO WANGGOOLBA CREEK	
TREES:	*Agathis robusta, Archontophoenix cunninghamiana, Schizomeria ovata*

VINES:	Embelia australiana, Flagellaria indica
SAPLINGS:	Alyxia ruscifolia, Araucaria bidwillii (planted), Endiandra discolor, Mischocarpus pyriformis

BOARDWALK ALONG WANGGOOLBA CREEK	
SAPLINGS/TREES:	Archontophoenix cunninghamiana, Beilschmiedia elliptica, Canarium australasicum, Syzygium luehmannii
SHRUBS:	Eupomatia laurina, Tasmannia insipida
VINES:	Dioscorea transversa, Flagellaria indica, Freycinetia scandens, Hypserpa decumbens, Pandorea jasminoides, Ripogonum discolor
TREE FERNS:	Angiopteris evecta, Dicksonia youngiae, Todea barbara
OTHER FERNS ALLIES:	Abrodictyum caudatum, Blechnum camfieldii, Blechnum cartilagineum, Lindsaea brachypoda, Psilotum nudum, Tmesipteris truncata
OTHER:	Cordyline spp., Cyperus pedunculosus

TABLE 9: List of plants commonly seen at Central Station.

Not all species are native to Central Station as many were planted by the Forestry Department and early forestry families that lived there. Some of the species planted include the *Araucaria cunninghamii* (hoop pine) and the small plot of *Eucalyptus grandis* (flooded gum) planted in 1950 near the entrance to the Wanggoolba Creek board walk [40].

A visit to Central Station is not complete without a trip down the walking track to the Wanggoolba Creek boardwalk. Here you can see the magnificent clear water flowing across the white sand and the ancient fern *Angiopteris evecta*, with its 7 to 8 metre fronds thought to be relatively unchanged for 250 million years.

Along the creek, the most abundant vine is the climbing pandanus, *Freycinetia scandens*. The area is the home of numerous palms, such as the *Archontophoenix cunninghamiana* and rainforest trees such as *Beilschmiedia elliptica* (brown walnut, a valuable timber species), *Canarium australasicum* (mango bark) and *Syzygium luehmannii* (small-leaved lillypilly), seen most easily when the tree produces its reddish-pink young leaves. Figure 7 provides a transverse cross-section of the island at Wanggoolba Creek through Central Station and the position of some of the plant species to be found there.

SITE 7. PILE VALLEY

The tall open (closed) forests at Pile Valley are dominated by a magnificent stand of giants, the *Syncarpia hillii* (satinay). These satinay trees are up to 40 metres in height with the area protected from timber harvesting since the 1930s, as is evidenced by the lack of tree stumps. *Gmelina leichhardtii* (white beech) is a co-dominant species also seen on this site.

Satinay is recognised by its thick furrowed bark, dark fleshy green leaves and a distinctive fruit which has seven capsules, with six coming from a central capsule, allowing for relatively easy identification. Satinay is almost confined to the island and when found elsewhere at Cooloola, or on Moreton Island, it is not as large.

While the trees in this stand are mainly satinay, this species is usually found in combination with *Lophostemon confertus* (brush box), commonly referred to as satinay-brush box forest. Brush box has light brown scaled lower bark with salmon pink coloured bark on branches and upper trunk.

Piper hederaceum is the prominent climbing vine on the *Syncarpia hillii* trees in Pile Valley. Other trees to 15 metres tall include *Schizomeria ovata*, while *Backhousia myrtifolia* (carrol) is the common understorey species to 10 metres. Carrol is a large tree or shrub with a dense conspicuous canopy that becomes leaner when grown in dense shade. Shrubs and small trees at this site include: the common and easily recognisable palm *Archontophoenix cunninghamiana*, *Cordyline* spp., *Neolitsea dealbata*, *Notelaea longifolia* and *Trochocarpa laurina*.

Ground cover comprises *Blechnum cartilagineum*, *Lomandra laxa*, and *Macrozamia douglasii*. The latter species which grows to about 2 metres high is not a palm but a cycad and belongs to a more primitive family of plants. It can be identified easily by the fruit located at its base, which is similar to a large green pineapple that turns bright orange when ripe. Vine species also found in the area include: *Callerya megasperma*, *Flagellaria indica*, *Ripogonum discolor* and the spiny *Smilax australis*.

Additional species along the edge of the road heading north from Pile Valley include: *Eupomatia laurina, Euroshinus falcatus,*

Glochidion lobocarpum, Litsea australis, Myrsine variabilis, Rhodamnia acuminata and *Wilkiea macrophylla.*

SITE 8. LAKE MCKENZIE (LAKE BOORANGOORA)

One of the 40 perched, sand dune lakes on the island, Lake McKenzie, is surrounded by white sandy beaches with mildly acidic water due to the release of organic acids from the rotting vegetation. The lake is a popular swimming destination.

The dominant tree species surrounding the lake is *Eucalyptus pilularis* (blackbutt), growing to between 20 and 25 metres high, with occasional smaller trees of *Syncarpia hillii* (satinay) present.

Understorey shrubs, 3 to 4 metres high, of *Banksia aemula, Dodonaea triquetra, Leptospermum polygalifolium, Leucopogon margarodes, Monotoca* sp.*, Phebalium woombye* and *Ricinocarpos pinifolius* are present. *Dodonaea triquetra* or large-leafed hop bush is found here and in many other vegetation associations throughout the island, especially in protected areas. *Dodonaea triquetra* has distinctive winged fruits which are usually green in colour, but can vary from pale pink to black. *Monotoca* sp. is a common understorey species which grows to 4 metres and has numerous branches often low to the ground, with very distinctive prickly pointed leaves and tiny green flowers.

Ground layer species, 1 to 2 m high, include: *Boronia rosmarinifolia, Caustis blakei, Cassytha pubescens, Lomandra laxa, Platysace lanceolata, Pteridium esculentum, Schizaea bifida* and the very striking *Xanthorrhoea macronema* (grass tree).

SITE 9. MCKENZIE JETTY

FORESTRY

The forests on Fraser Island / K'gari were first logged for conifers (*Agathis robusta* and *Araucaria cunninghamii*) in 1863 by Yankee Jack Piggot and the Hines family from Maryborough[39]. Logging operations ceased in 1991 at which time the island was nominated for World Heritage Listing. Initially, the logging was largely ad hoc, until 1913 when the Forestry Department began to implement logging guidelines.

Until the mid-1930s all logging was undertaken with bullock teams and steam trains. They hauled the logs to the west coast, from where they were floated or barged to Maryborough for processing into boards.

Hardwood species, dominated by *Eucalyptus microcorys* (tallowwood) and blackbutt, were harvested as the conifer stands dwindled. They were most sought after up to the mid-1960s, when most of the logging operations still used bullock teams and steam trains [39]. After the introduction of skidding machines and log trucks in the 1970s, other species such as *Syncarpia hillii* and *Lophostemon confertus* were harvested.

In 1919 Hepburn McKenzie, a successful New South Wales timber merchant, built a sawmill at White Cliffs on the west coast, just south of what is now the Kingfisher Bay Resort. The company constructed a tramline from the mill at McKenzie Jetty to Lake McKenzie, with two branch lines spreading out from the lake. The tramlines were steel-railed and the log bogies were pulled by a steam engine. McKenzie's mill was auctioned off in 1925 and the tramway and wharf (which is still partly standing today), were sold to the Queensland Forestry Board. The Forestry Department, as it became, stopped milling operations in 1935 and sold the rails from McKenzie's tramway and the locomotive in 1941 [34 40].

Most of the vegetation communities on Fraser Island / K'gari (except rainforests) can survive fire and reproduce through their adaptation characteristics such as presence of thick bark, ability to coppice or develop epicormic shoots, or from seed fall and rapid seedling growth once germinated.

Fire was an integral part of life for the Aboriginal communities on the island. Later the Queensland Department of Forestry continued using fire to reduce fuel in the forests, encourage the regeneration of blackbutt forests and manage other vegetation types, such as the wallum. Fuel reduction prescribed burning was implemented over large tracts of the island to reduce forest fuel loads which reduces the risk of uncontrolled wildfires in the hot dry months. This practice, used by the Aboriginal communities prior to the 1800s, was adapted by the Queensland Parks and Wildlife Service, which currently manages most of the island.

Forest harvesting operations managed by the Queensland Department of Forestry prior to 1991, were subject to controls on the operations to minimise site disturbance. Tree selection was undertaken to determine the number, size and direction of fall of the trees in the satinay-brush box forests with over-mature trees remaining.

Blackbutt was harvested in small coupes which were subsequently burned, as blackbutt requires a higher level of site disturbance to regenerate successfully, compared to the satinay-brush box, whose remaining trees take advantage of the small canopy openings created by the harvesting operations to form the future forest. Most of the extensive blackbutt forests and satiny-brush box forests seen on the island today resulted from these silviculture practices or from very early fires or major disturbances. Many of the large trees seen today which are over 2.5 metres in diameter most likely resulted from pre-European fires and are estimated to be over 500 years old.

Z-FORCE

During World War II, a special operations unit was formed in 1942 to gather military intelligence, carry out covert operations and train resistance fighters from countries to the north of Australia that were occupied by Japanese forces. The unit was known as Z Special Unit.

Its Australian based training and operational schools included the Fraser Commando School, with camps at McKenzie Jetty and Central Station. In 1945, the McKenzie Jetty Commando School was a sizeable operation, with power, a water-pumping plant, a cinema, post office, library, hospital, lecture rooms, mess, canteens and accommodation for 100 trainees and a concrete relief map which can still be seen today.

The most famous of 'Z Force' operations was Operation Jaywick in September 1943, when a small force of 14 commandos raided Japanese shipping in Singapore Harbour. They motored up towards Singapore from Australia in the 'Krait' and then paddled into the harbour on the night of 26 September 1943 and placed limpet mines on several Japanese ships (weighing over 39,000 tons), seven of which either sank or were seriously damaged. Z Force mounted a second attack on Singapore Harbour, called Operation Rimau [41].

SITE 10. LAKE WABBY LOOKOUT

The forest in the vicinity of the lake Wabby Lookout is dominated by *Allocasuarina torulosa* (forest oak), *Angophora leiocarpa*, *Eucalyptus siderophloia*, *Eucalyptus racemosa* and *Lophostemon confertus*.

From the lookout, there is a short 1.5 hour walk downhill to the beach. Alternatively, a short drive north takes you to Cornwell's Break, then down to the beach and south to One Tree Rocks, located at the end of the Lake Wabby walking track.

Woodland vegetation dominated by *Casuarina equisetifolia* var. *incana* occurs on the dunes adjacent to the ocean beach, at the end of the walking track. Other species commonly seen along the walking track are listed in Table 10. Species in the wet soakage areas within the dunes are listed in Table 11.

SPECIES IN WOODLAND VEGETATION	
TREES:	*Banksia integrifolia, Casuarina equisetifolia* var. *incana*
SHRUBS:	*Alyxia ruscifolia*
GRASSES:	*Eragrostis interrupta, Ischaemum triticeum, Zoysia macrantha*
SEDGES:	*Carex pumila*
HERBS:	*Carpobrotus glaucescens, Ipomoea pes-caprae,*
	Poranthera microphylla, Dianella caerulea, Scaevola calendulacea
VINES:	*Hibbertia scandens*

TABLE 10: Species seen on the walking track from Lake Wabby lookout to the beach.

SPECIES NAMES	
APIACEAE	*Centella asiatica*
ASTERACEAE	*Coronidium oxylepis, Sphaeromorphaea australis*
CAMPANULACEAE	*Lobelia anceps*
CYPERACEAE	*Cyperus polystachyos, Eleocharis difformis,*
	Eleocharis sphacelata, Fimbristylis nutans
ERIOCAULACEAE	*Eriocaulon scariosum*
JUNCAGINACEAE	*Triglochin striata*
LENTIBULARIACEAE	*Utricularia gibba, Utricularia lateriflora*
MELASTOMACEAE	*Melastoma malabathricum*
MENYANTHACEAE	*Nymphoides exiliflora*
PHILYDRACEAE	*Philydrum lanuginosum*
PLANTAGINACEAE	*Bacopa monnieri*
POACEAE	*Paspalum scrobiculatum*

TABLE 11: Species in the soakage areas.

LIST OF PLANT SPECIES FOUND ON FRASER ISLAND / K'GARI

This is a comprehensive list of over 850 species and 147 families of flowering plants and ferns. The genera and species are tabulated alphabetically, according to the family in which they occur and include common names where known.

The collections and observations of species which make up the list were compiled by the author from recent visits to the island and from his initial collections between 1979 and 1981, whilst undertaking research on the island with the University of New England and the Department of Forestry, Queensland. The other sources of information used to compile the species list are from collections as follows:

- Queensland Department of Forestry (1979) Revegetation Studies on Sand Mined Areas -Fraser Island. Dept. of Forestry Queensland. (unpublished.)
- Applegate, G.B. (1982) Biomass of Blackbutt Forests on Fraser Island MSc Thesis, University of New England. Check list of 650 plant species and 143 families prepared during the field work on Fraser Island between 1979-1981.
- Baxter, Pamela H., (1968) Vegetation notes on Fraser Island Queensland Naturalist 19: 11-20.
- Blake, S.T., (1968) The plants and plant communities of Fraser, Moreton and Stradbroke Island. Queensland Naturalist 19: 23-30.
- Cribb, A.B., (1974) Additions to the rain forest flora of Fraser Island. Queensland Naturalist 21: (1-2): 13-14.
- Elsol, J.A.E. and G.B. Applegate (1981) Field Trip 14, Fraser Island XIII Botanical Congress. Check list prepared during the preparation for a field trip to Fraser Island.
- McDonald W.J.F., (1988) Vegetation Survey of Fraser Island Rainforests. Department of Forestry, Queensland.
- Queensland Herbarium Records for Fraser Island, (2019).

All species in the species list have been verified by the Queensland Herbarium, Brisbane.

The species have been sorted and placed into nine vegetation associations based on vegetation structure, where they are most likely to be seen and in the particular landform or physiographic unit.

The physiographic units are:

- Strand
- Fore Dune
- Hind Dune
- High Dune
- Littoral Flats

The vegetation associations are:

- Grasslands
- Sedgeland
- Herbland
- Low Woodland
- Low Open Forest
- Heath
- Woodland
- Open Forest
- Closed Forest

The plants in the species list are identified by the Status (*-introduced and E-endangered) and their Habit according to the following definitions:

T	Tree, or woody plant more than 5 m high and usually has one stem
S	Shrub or woody plant less than 5 m high, usually with more than one stem arising from near ground level
PS	Parasitic Shrub is a shrub living on another plant and obtaining nourishment from the host plant
P	Palm
H	Herb, non woody plant
AH	Aquatic Herb
TH	Tufted Herb
SH	Succulent Herb
RH	Rhizomatous Herb
V	Vine
PV	Parasitic Vine
E	Epiphyte plant living on another plant but not obtaining nourishment from that plant
TF	Tree Fern

PLANT SPECIES LIST

PLANT FAMILY: SPECIES: COMMON NAME

BOTANICAL NAME	COMMON NAME
ACANTHACEAE	
Avicennia marina subsp. *australasica* (Walp.) J.Everett	grey mangrove
Harnieria hygrophiloides (F.Muell.) R.M.Baker	white karambal
Pseuderanthemum variabile (R. Br.) Radlk.	pastal flower
AIZOACEAE	
Carpobrotus aequilaterus (Haw.) N.E.Brown	noon flower
Carpobrotus glaucescens (Haw.) Schwantes	pig face
Sesuvium portulacastrum (L.) L.	sea purslane
Tetragonia tetragonoides (Pall.) Kuntze	New Zealand spinach
AMARANTHACEAE	
Achyranthes aspera L.	chaff flower
Gomphrena celosioides Mart.	soft kharkiweed
Guilleminea densa (Humb. & Bonpl. ex Schult.) Moq.	small matweed
AMARYLLIDACEAE	
Clivia sp.	lily
Crinum pedunculatum R.Br.	swamp lilly
ANACARDIACEAE	
Euroshinus falcatus Hook.f.	ribbon wood
Pleiogynium timorense (DC.) Leenh.	Burdekin plum
ANNONACEAE	
Melodorum leichhardtii (F.Muell.) Benth.	zig zag vine
Polyalthia nitidissima (Dunal) Benth.	canary beech
APIACEAE	
Apium prostratum Labill. ex Vent.	sea celery
Centella asiatica (L.) Urb.	pennywort
Cyclospermum leptophyllum (Pers.) Sprague ex Britton & P.Wilson	
Platysace ericoides (Sieber ex Spreng.) C.Norman	shrubby platysace
Platysace lanceolata (Labill.) Druce	heath platysace

STATUS	GRASS LAND	SEDGE LAND	HERB LAND	LOW WOOD LAND	LOW OPEN FOREST	HEATH	WOOD LAND	OPEN FOREST	CLOSED FOREST
				T					
								H	H
									H
			SH						
			SH						
			H		H				
			H						
*			H						
*			H						
*			H						
*								H	
			H						
					T			T	
				T	T			T	
					V			V	
				T	T				
	H	H							
			H						
*					H			H	
			S						
					S	S	S	S	

BOTANICAL NAME	COMMON NAME
Platysace linearifolia (Cav.) C.Norman	narrow-leaf platysace
Xanthosia pilosa Rudge	wooly xanthosia
APOCYNACEAE	
Alyxia ruscifolia R.Br.	chain fruit
Asclepias curassavica L.	red-head cottonbush
Cynanchum carnosum (R. Br.) Merr.& Rolfe	mangrove waxflower vine
Gomphocarpus physocarpus E.Mey.	balloon cotton bush
Hoya australis R.Br. ex Traill subsp. *australis*	hoya
Marsdenia fraseri Benth.	narrow-leafed milk vine
Marsdenia glandulifera C.T.White	monkey rope
Marsdenia rostrata R.Br.	milk vine
Melodinus australis (F.Muell.) Pierre	rubber vine
Parsonsia latifolia F.Muell.	green-leaved silkpod
Parsonsia straminea (R.Br.) F.Muell.	monkey vine
Parsonsia velutina R.Br.	
Parsonsia ventricosa F.Muell.	pointed silk pod
ARALIACEAE	
Astrotricha glabra Domin	
Astrotricha longifolia Benth.	star hair brush
Cephalaralia cephalobotrys (F.Muell.) Harms.	climbing panax
Hydrocotyle acutiloba (F.Muell.) N.A.Wakef.	pennywort
Hydrocotyle bonariensis Lam.	pennywort
Hydrocotyle verticillata Thunb.	pennywort
Polyscias australiana (F.Muell.) Philipson	ivory basswood
Polyscias elegans (C.Moore & F.Muell.) Harms	celerywood
Trachymene incisa Rudge subsp. *incisa*	wild parsnip
ARAUCARIACEAE	
Agathis robusta (C.Moore ex F.Muell.) F.M.Bailey	South Qld kauri pine
Araucaria bidwillii Hook	bunya pine

| STATUS | STRAND | LITTORAL FLAT | FORE DUNE | HIND DUNE | HIGH DUNE | | | | |
	GRASS LAND	SEDGE LAND	HERB LAND	LOW WOOD LAND	LOW OPEN FOREST	HEATH	WOOD LAND	OPEN FOREST	CLOSED FOREST
			S			S			
					S	S			
					S		S	S	
				H				H	
					V			V	
*			S			S			
			V		V			V	
		V					V	V	
							V	V	
							V	V	
								V	V
					V		V	V	
			V		V		V	V	
									V
					V			V	
					S	S	S	S	
					S	S	S	S	
									V
							H	H	
				H			H		
							H		
					T			T	
					T			T	
				H	H		H		
								T	T
*								T	

78

BOTANICAL NAME	COMMON NAME
Araucaria cunninghamii Mudie var. *cunninghamii*	hoop pine
ARECACEAE	
Archontophoenix cunninghamiana (H.Wendl.) H.Wendl. & Drude	piccabeen palm
Linospadix monostachyos (Mart.) H.Wendl.	walking stick palm
Livistona australis (B.Br.) Mart.	cabbage tree palm
Livistona decora (W.Bull) Dowe	
ARECEAE	
Gymnostachys anceps R.Br.	settler's flax
ASPLENIACEAE	
Asplenium australasicum (J.Sm.) Hook.	crows nest fern
Asplenium polyodon G.Forst.	mare's tail fern
ASTERACEAE	
Acanthospermum hispidum DC.	star burr
Actites megalocarpus (Hook. f.) Lander	beach sow thistle
Ageratum conyzoides L.	billygoat weed
Bidens pilosa L.	cobbler's pegs
Bidens pilosa L. var. *pilosa*	cobbler's pegs
Chrysanthemoides monilifera subsp. *rotundata* (DC.) Norl.	bitou bush
Chrysocephalum apiculatum (Labill.) Steetz	yellow buttons
Cirsium vulgare (Savi) Ten	common thistle
Conyza canadensis (L.) Crong.	canadian fleabane
Conyza parva Cronquist	
Conyza sumatrensis (Retz.) E.Walker	tall fleabane
Coronidium elatum (A.Cunn. ex DC.) Paul G.Wilson subsp. *elatum*	
Coronidium oxylepis subsp. *carnosum* Paul G.Wilson	everlasting daisy
Crassocephalum crepidioides (Benth.) S.Moore	thickhead
Cyanthillium cinereum (L.) H.Rob.	vernonia

			STRAND	LITTORAL FLAT	FORE DUNE	HIND DUNE	HIGH DUNE		
STATUS	GRASS LAND	SEDGE LAND	HERB LAND	LOW WOOD LAND	LOW OPEN FOREST	HEATH	WOOD LAND	OPEN FOREST	CLOSED FOREST
								T	T
									P
									P
				P	P				
				P	P				
					H		H		
									E
									E
*				H	H				
			H						
*			H						
*			H	H	H				
*			H	H	H				
*			H	H	H				
					H			H	
				H	H				
*			H	H	H				
*			H	H	H				
*			H	H	H				
			H		H			H	
			H		H		H	H	
*			H	H	H				
					H			H	

80

BOTANICAL NAME	COMMON NAME
Eclipta prostrata (L.) L.	white elipta
Emilia sonchifolia (L.) DC. var. *sonchifolia*	sunflower
Emilia sonchifolia var. *javanica* (Burm.f.) Mattf.	sunflower
Enydra woolsii F.Muell.	love grass
Erechtites valerianifolius forma *valerianifolius* (Link ex Spreng.) DC.	Brazilian fireweed
Erigeron pusillus Nutt.	horseweed
Erigeron sumatrensis Retz.	tall fleabane
Galinsoga parviflora Cav.	potato weed
Gamochaeta pensylvanica (Willd.) Cabrera	cudweed
Glossocardia bidens (Retz.) Veldkamp	native cobbler's peggs
Picris angustifolia subsp. *carolorum-henricorum* (Lack) S.Holzapfel	
Podolepis arachnoidea (Hook.) Druce	clustered copper-wire daisy
Podolepis longipedata A.Cunn. ex DC.	tall copper-wired daisy
Podolepis neglecta G.L.Davis	pololepis
Praxelis clematidea R.M.King & H.Rob.	mistflower
Pseudognaphalium luteoalbum (L.) Hilliard & B.L.Burtt	jersey cudweed
Pterocaulon redolens (Willd.) Fern.-Vill.	
Senecio pinnatifolius A.Rich.var. *pinnatifolius*	variable groundsel
Sigesbeckia orientalis L.	Indian weed
Soliva sessilis Ruiz & Pav.	bindy
Sonchus oleraceus L.	common sowthistle
Sphaeromorphaea australis (Less.) Kitam.	spreading nutheads
Sphagneticola trilobata (L.) Pruski	Singapore daisy
Symphyotrichum subulatum (Michx.) G.L.Nesom	wild aster
Wollastonia uniflora (Willd.) Orchard	yellow eclipta
Xerochrysum bracteatum (Vent.) Tzvelev	golden everlasting daisy

	STRAND								
		LITTORAL FLAT							
			FORE DUNE						
				HIND DUNE					
					HIGH DUNE				
STATUS	GRASS LAND	SEDGE LAND	HERB LAND	LOW WOOD LAND	LOW OPEN FOREST	HEATH	WOOD LAND	OPEN FOREST	CLOSED FOREST
*			H						
*			H	H	H				
*			H	H	H				
		H							
*						H			
*					F				
*				F					
			H	H	H				
*			H	H	H				
			H						
			H						
			H						
			H						
			H						
*			H	H					
			H	H					
			H	H					
					H	H			
			H	H	H				
*			H	H					
*			H		H				
		H	H		H				
*			H	H	H				
*			H				H		
			H						
			H	H	H				

BOTANICAL NAME	COMMON NAME
BIGNONIACEAE	
Pandorea floribunda (A.Cunn.ex DC.) Guymer	wonga wonga vine
Pandorea jasminoides (Lindl.) K.Schum.	scrub wonga vine
Tecomanthe hillii (F.Muell.) Steenis	Fraser Island creeper
BLANDFORDIACEAE	
Blandfordia grandiflora R.Br.	Christmas bells
BLECHNACEAE	
Blechnum camfieldii Tindale	
Blechnum cartilagineum Sw.	gristle fern
Blechnum indicum Burm. F.	
Pteridoblechnum neglectum (F.M.Bailey) Hennipman	
BRASSICACEAE	
Brassica tournefortii Gouan	Asian mustard
Cakile edentula (Bigelow) Hook.	sea rocket
Lepidium bonariense L.	Argentine peppercress
Lepidium virginicum L.	Virginian peppercress
BURMANNIACEAE	
Burmannia disticha L.	forked burmannia
BURSERACEAE	
Canarium australasicum (F.M.Bailey) Leenh.	mango bark
CACTACEAE	
Opuntia stricta (Haw.) Haw.	common prickly pear
CAESALPINACEAE	
Senna pendula var. *glabrata* (Vogel) H.S.Irwin & Barneby	
Caesalpinia bonduc (L.) Roxb.	nicker bean
Chamaecrista nomame (Siebold) H.Ohashi	dwarf cassia
CAMPANULACEAE	
Lobelia anceps L.f.	angled lobelia
Lobelia purpurascens R.Br.	white root

| STATUS | STRAND | LITTORAL FLAT | | FORE DUNE | HIND DUNE | HIGH DUNE | | | |
	GRASS LAND	SEDGE LAND	HERB LAND	LOW WOOD LAND	LOW OPEN FOREST	HEATH	WOOD LAND	OPEN FOREST	CLOSED FOREST
					V			V	V
					V			V	V
E								V	V
E						H			
		H				H			
								H	H
		H						H	
								H	H
*							H	H	
*		H	H						
*		H	H						
*		H	H						
		H							
								T	T
*			SH		SH				
					S				
								S	
								S	
		H	H						
							H		

84

BOTANICAL NAME	COMMON NAME
Lobelia trigonocaulis F.Muell.	forest lobelia
Wahlenbergia stricta (R.Br.) Sweet	Australian blue bell
CAROPHYLLACEAE	
Cerastium glomeratum Thuillier	mouse ear chickweed
Polycarpon tetraphyllum (L.) L.	four-leaf allseed
Silene gallica L.	common catchfly
Stellaria media (L.) Vill.	chickweed
CARPODETACEAE	
Abrophyllum ornans (F.Muell.) Hook.f. ex Benth. var. *ornans*	native hydrangea
CASUARINACEAE	
Allocasuarina littoralis (Salisb.) L.A.S.Johnson	black she oak
Allocasuarina torulosa (Aiton) L.A.S.Johnson	forest oak
Casuarina equisetifolia subsp. *incana* (Benth.) L.A.S.Johnson	coastal she oak
Casuarina glauca Sieber ex Spreng.	swamp oak
CELASTRACEAE	
Denhamia celastroides (F.Muell.) Jessup	broad-leaved boxwood
Hippocratea barbata F.Muell.	knotvine
CENTROLEPIDACEAE	
Centrolepis exserta (R.Br.) Roem. & Schult.	centrolepis
Centrolepis strigosa (R.Br.) Roem. & Schult.	
CHENOPODIACEAE	
Dysphania ambrosiodes L.	wormseed
Suaeda arbusculoides L.S.Sm.	jellybean plant
Suaeda australis (R.Br.) Moq.	seablite
Tecticornia halocnemoides (Nees) K.A. Sheph. & Paul G.Wilson	blackseed samphire
Tecticornia indica subsp. *leiostachya* (Benth.) K.A.Sheph. & Paul G.Wilson	samphire
CLUSIACEAE	
Calophyllum inophyllum L.	beach calophyllum

		STRAND							
		LITTORAL FLAT							
		FORE DUNE							
		HIND DUNE							
		HIGH DUNE							
STATUS	GRASS LAND	SEDGE LAND	HERB LAND	LOW WOOD LAND	LOW OPEN FOREST	HEATH	WOOD LAND	OPEN FOREST	CLOSED FOREST
								H	
			H						
*				F					
					S				
			H		H				
*				F			F		
									T
							T	T	
								T	
			T		T				
				T			T		
								T	
								V	V
			H						
							H		
*			H		H		H		
			SH						
			SH						
			SH						
			SH						
	T								

86

BOTANICAL NAME	COMMON NAME
Hypericum gramineum G.Forst.	small st johns wort
COLCHICACEAE	
Burchardia umbellata R.Br.	milk maids
Gloriosa superba L.	glory lilly
COMBRETACEAE	
Lumnitzera racemosa Willd.	black mangrove
COMMELINACEAE	
Commelina diffusa Burm.f.	scurvy weed
CONVOLVULACEAE	
Calystegia soldanella R.Br.	sea bind weed
Evolvulus alsinoides (L.) L.	baby blue eyes
Ipomoea cairica (L.) Sweet	morning glory
Ipomoea littoralis Blume	
Ipomoea pes-caprae subsp. *brasiliensis* (L.) Ooststr.	goat's foot
Polymeria calycina R.Br.	pink trumpet flower
CUNONIACEAE	
Bauera capitata Ser. ex DC.	clustered bauera
Schizomeria ovata D.Don	crabapple
CUPRESSACEAE	
Callitris columellaris F.Muell.	white cypress pine
Callitris macleayana (F.Muell.) F.Muell.	stringy bark cypress pine
Callitris rhomboidea R.Br. ex Rich.	dune cypress pine
CYATHEACEAE	
Cyathea cooperi (Hook. ex F.Muell.) Domin	
Cyathea leichhardtiana (F.Muell.) Copel.	prickly tree fern
CYMODOEACEAE	
Halodule uninervis (Forssk.) Asch.	sea grass
CYPERACEAE	
Baumea arthrophylla (Nees) Boeckeler	

STATUS	GRASS LAND	SEDGE LAND	HERB LAND	LOW WOOD LAND	LOW OPEN FOREST	HEATH	WOOD LAND	OPEN FOREST	CLOSED FOREST
			H	H	H	H	H	H	H
		H							
			H						
				T					
			H	H	H				
	V		V						
			H		H		H	H	
	H		H						
		H							
		H	H						
	H		H						
						S			
									T
					T		T		
								T	
				T					
									TF
									TF
			H						
					RH				

Landform zones across the top (spanning the vegetation columns): STRAND, LITTORAL FLAT, FORE DUNE, HIND DUNE, HIGH DUNE

88

BOTANICAL NAME	COMMON NAME
Baumea articulata (R.Br.) S.T.Blake	jointed twigrush
Baumea juncea (R.Br.) Palla	bare twigrush
Baumea muelleri (C.B.Clarke) S.T.Blake	twigrush
Baumea rubiginosa (Spreng.) Boeckeler	soft twigrush
Baumea teretifolia (R.Br.) Palla	twigrush
Bulbostylis barbata (Rottb.) C.B.Clarke	
Carex pumila Thunb.	strand sedge
Caustis blakei Kuek. subsp. *blakei*	foxtail
Caustis recurvata Spreng.	curly wigs
Cladium procerum S.T.Blake	leafy twigbush
Cyperus brevifolius (Rottb.) Endl.ex Hassk.	sedge
Cyperus conicus (R.Br.) Boeckeler	sedge
Cyperus cyperoides (L.) Kuntze	sedge
Cyperus eglobosus K.L.Wilson	sedge
Cyperus enervis R.Br.	sedge
Cyperus haspan L.	sedge
Cyperus laevigatus L.	sedge
Cyperus lucidus R.Br.	sedge
Cyperus pedunculosus F.Muell.	sedge
Cyperus polystachyos Rottb. var. *polystachyos*	bunchy sedge
Cyperus scaber (R.Br.) Boeckeler	sedge
Cyperus stoloniferus Retz.	sedge
Cyperus stradbrokensis Domin	sedge
Eleocharis cylindrostachys Boeckeler	rush
Eleocharis difformis S.T.Blake	rush
Eleocharis equisetina C.Presl	spike rush
Eleocharis geniculata (L.) Roem. & Schult.	spike rush
Eleocharis ochrostachys Steud.	rush
Eleocharis sphacelata R.Br.	tall spike rush

STATUS	GRASS LAND	SEDGE LAND	HERB LAND	LOW WOOD LAND	LOW OPEN FOREST	HEATH	WOOD LAND	OPEN FOREST	CLOSED FOREST
								HIGH DUNE	
						HIND DUNE			
				FORE DUNE					
			LITTORAL FLAT						
		STRAND							
		RH							
		RH							
		RH							
		RH							
		RH							
		TH	TH						
		RH	RH						
					H		H	H	
						H			
		H	H						
					H	H	H	H	
					H	H	H	H	
					H	H	H	H	
					H	H	H	H	
					TH	TH	TH	TH	
				H	H	H	H		
					H		H	H	
					H		H	H	
								H	H
			H	H	H		H	H	
			H		H	H			
	H		H						
			H	H			H	H	
		H							
		H							
		H							
		H							
		H	H				H		
		H	H						

90

BOTANICAL NAME	COMMON NAME
Ficinia nodosa (Rottb.) Goetgh., Muasya, & D.A.Simpson	knotty club rush
Fimbristylis dichotoma (L.) Vahl	common finger rush
Fimbristylis ferruginea (L.) Vahl	rush
Fimbristylis nutans (Retz.) Vahl	rush
Fimbristylis polytrichoides (Retz.) R.Br.	rush
Gahnia clarkei Benl	tall sword grass
Gahnia sieberiana Kunth	sword grass
Lepidosperma laterale R.Br.	sword sedge
Lepidosperma longitudinale Labill.	pithy swod sedge
Lepironia articulata (Retz.) Domin	grey rush
Schoenoplectus tabernaemontani (C.C.Gmel.) Palla	clubrush
Schoenus apogon Roem. & Schult. var. *apogon*	fluke bogrush
Schoenus brevifolius R.Br.	bogrush
Schoenus calostachyus (R.Br.) Roem. & Schult.	bogrush
Schoenus melanostachys R.Br.	rifle grass
Schoenus nitens (R.Br.) Roem. & Schult.	shiny bogrush
Schoenus ornithopodioides (Kuek.) S.T. Blake	bogrush
Schoenus paludosus (R.Br.) Roem. & Schult.	bogrush
Schoenus scabripes Benth.	bogrush
Trachystylis stradbrokensis (Domin) Kuek.	
DENNSTAEDTIACEAE	
Histiopteris incisa (Thunb.) J.Sm.	bats-wing fern
Pteridium esculentum (G.Forst.) Cockayne	common bracken fern
DICKSONIACEAE	
Calochlaena dubia (R.Br.) M.D.Turner & R.A.White	false bracken fern
Dicksonia youngiae C.Moore ex Baker	bristly tree fern
DILLENIACEAE	
Hibbertia acicularis (Labill.) F.Muell.	prickly guinea flower
Hibbertia fasciculata R.Br.	bundled guinea flower

STATUS	STRAND	LITTORAL FLAT	FORE DUNE	HIND DUNE		HIGH DUNE			
	GRASS LAND	SEDGE LAND	HERB LAND	LOW WOOD LAND	LOW OPEN FOREST	HEATH	WOOD LAND	OPEN FOREST	CLOSED FOREST
			TH			TH			
		H	H				H•		
		H	H				H		
					H		H	H	
		H			H		H	H	
						H	H		
		H				H			
				H	H		H	H	
				H	H		H	H	
		RH			RH			RH	
		H							
		H							
		H				H			
		H				H			
		H·							
		H							
		H							
		H		H			H	H	
		H		H			H	H	
							H	H	
									H
				H	H		H	H	
								H	
									TF
					S			S	
					S	S		S	

BOTANICAL NAME	COMMON NAME
Hibbertia linearis R.Br. ex DC.	guinea flower
Hibbertia linearis var. *floribunda* Benth.	showy guinea flower
Hibbertia salicifolia (DC.) F.Muell.	willow guinea flower
Hibbertia scandens (Willd.) Gilg	snake vine
Hibbertia stricta (DC.) R.Br. ex F.Muell.	erect guinea flower
Hibbertia vestita A.Cunn. ex Benth. *var.* vestita	hairy guinea flower
DIOSCOREACEAE	
Dioscorea transversa R.Br.	native yam
DROSERACEAE	
Drosera binata Labill.	fork sundew
Drosera finlaysoniana Wall. ex Arn.	sundew
Drosera lunata Buch.Ham. ex DC.	pale sundew
Drosera pygmaea DC.	sundew
Drosera spatulata Labill.	spoon leaved sundew
Drosera spatulata var. *spatulata* Labill.	spoon leaved sundew
EBENACEAE	
Diospyros pentamera (Woolls & F.Muell.) F.Muell.	black ebony
ELAEOCARPACEAE	
Elaeocarpus eumundi F.M.Bailey	Eumundi quandong
Elaeocarpus grandis F.Muell.	blue quandong
Elaeocarpus obovatus G.Don	blueberry ash
Elaeocarpus reticulatus Sm.	ash quandong
Tetratheca thymifolia Sm.	black-eyed susan
ERICACEAE	
Acrotriche aggregata R.Br.	tall ground berry
Agiortia pedicellata C.T.White Quinn	wallum bearded heath
Brachyloma daphnoides (Sm.) Benth. subsp. *daphnoides*	daphne heath
Brachyloma scortechinii F.Muell.	daphne heath
Epacris microphylla R.Br. var. *microphylla*	coral heath

| STATUS | STRAND | | | LITTORAL FLAT | FORE DUNE | HIND DUNE | HIGH DUNE | | |
	GRASS LAND	SEDGE LAND	HERB LAND	LOW WOOD LAND	LOW OPEN FOREST	HEATH	WOOD LAND	OPEN FOREST	CLOSED FOREST
					S			S	
					S			S	
						S			
			V		V				
					S		S	S	
				S	S	S	S	S	
					V		V	V	
		H					H	H	
		H							
		H							
		H							
		H							
		H							
									T
									T
									T
									T
					T		T	T	T
				S		S			
					S			S	
					S	S			
					S	S			
					S	S			
					S				

BOTANICAL NAME	COMMON NAME
Epacris obtusifolia Sm.	common heath
Epacris pulchella Cav.	wallum heath
Leucopogon leptospermoides R.Br.	tree bearded heath
Leucopogon margarodes R.Br.	pearl bearded heath
Leucopogon parviflorus (Andrews) Lindl.	coast bearded heath
Leucopogon pimeleoides A.Cunn. ex DC.	feathered bearded heath
Monotoca scoparia (Sm.) R.Br.	prickly broom heath
Monotoca sp. (Fraser Island P.Baxter 777)	Fraser Island broom heath
Sprengelia sprengelioides (R.Br.) Druce	sprengela
Styphelia viridis subsp. *breviflora* (Benth.) J.M.Powell	green five corners
Trochocarpa laurina (R.Br. ex Rudge) R.Br.	tree heath
Woollsia pungens (Cav.) F.Muell.	woolsia
ERIOCAULACEAE	
Eriocaulon australe R.Br.	pipewort
Eriocaulon scariosum Sm.	pipewort
EUPHORBIACEAE	
Claoxylon australe Baill. ex Muell.Arg.	brittlewood
Euphorbia cyathophora Murr.	
Euphorbia hyssopifolia L.	
Excoecaria agallocha L.	blind your-eye mangrove
Homalanthus populifolius Graham	native bleeding heat
Ricinocarpos pinifolius Desf.	wedding bush
EUPOMATIACEAE	
Eupomatia bennettii F.Muell.	small bolwarra
Eupomatia laurina R.Br.	bolwarra
FABACEAE	
Abrus precatorius subsp. *africanus* Verdc.	crabs eye creeper
Aotus ericoides (Vent.) G.Don	common aotus
Aotus lanigera A.Cunn. ex Benth.	pointed aotus

| STATUS | STRAND | | LITTORAL FLAT | FORE DUNE | HIND DUNE | HIGH DUNE | | | |
	GRASS LAND	SEDGE LAND	HERB LAND	LOW WOOD LAND	LOW OPEN FOREST	HEATH	WOOD LAND	OPEN FOREST	CLOSED FOREST
					S				
					S				
							S	S	
					S		S	S	
					S		S	S	
					S		S	S	
					S		S	S	
					S		S	S	
						S			
						S			
							T	T	T
						S			
		H							
		H					H		
								S	S
*				S					
*					H		H	H	
					T				
					T		T	T	
						S	S	S	
									S
									S
*				S					
						S	S		
						S	S		

BOTANICAL NAME	COMMON NAME
Austrosteenisia blackii (F.Muell.) R. Geesink var. *blackii*	blood vine
Bossiaea brownii Benth.	downy bossiaea
Bossiaea concolor (Maiden & Betche) I.Thomps.	appressed bossiaea
Bossiaea ensata Sieber ex DC.	leafless bossiaea
Bossiaea heterophylla Vent.	variable bossieea
Bossiaea rupicola A.Cunn. ex Benth.	pea flower
Callerya megasperma (F.Muell.) Schot	native wisteria
Canavalia rosea (Sw.) DC.	coastal jack bean
Crotalaria brevis Domin	rattlepod
Crotalaria pallida var. *obovata* (G.Don) Polhill	streaked rattlepod
Daviesia acicularis Sm.	bitter pea
Daviesia umbellulata Sm.	bitter pea
Desmodium nemorosum F.Muell. ex Benth.	wild pea
Dillwynia floribunda Sm.	showy parrot pea
Dillwynia retorta (J.C.Wendl.) Druce	hairy parrot pea
Glycine clandestina J.C.Wendl. var. clandestina	twining glycine
Glycine tabacina (Labill.) Benth.	glycine pea
Glycine tomentella Hayata	woolly glycine
Gompholobium latifolium Sm.	broad wedge pea
Gompholobium pinnatum Sm.	poor man's gold
Gompholobium virgatum Sieber ex DC.	wallum wedge pea
Hardenbergia violacea (Schneev.) Stearn	native sarsaparilla vine
Hovea acutifolia A.Cunn. ex G.Don	pointed-leaf hovea
Hovea clavata I.Thomps.	Wide Bay hovea
Hovea similis I.Thomps.	purple bush pea
Indogofera hirsuta L.	
Jacksonia scoparia R.Br.	dogwood
Jacksonia stackhousei F.Muell.	wallum dogwood
Kennedia rubicunda (Schneev.) Vent.	dusky coral pea

| STATUS | STRAND | LITTORAL FLAT | FORE DUNE | HIND DUNE | HIGH DUNE | | | | |
	GRASS LAND	SEDGE LAND	HERB LAND	LOW WOOD LAND	LOW OPEN FOREST	HEATH	WOOD LAND	OPEN FOREST	CLOSED FOREST
						S	S		
					S		S		
							S		
					S	S	S		
						S			
						S	S		
								V	V
			H						
*			H						
*			H						
						S			
						S	S	S	
								S	S
					S		S	S	
					S	S	S	S	
			H						
			H				H		
							H	H	
								S	
						S		S	
					S	S	S	S	
					V		V	V	
								S	
							S	S	
							S	S	
*				S					
				S	S			S	
						S	S		
				V	V	V		V	

BOTANICAL NAME	COMMON NAME
Lotononis bainesii Baker	lotononis
Macroptilium atropurpureum (DC.) Urb.	siratro
Mezoneuron scortechinii F.Muell.	large pricklevine
Mirbelia rubiifolia (Andrews) G.Don	heathy mirbelia
Mucuna gigantea (Willd.) DC.	velvet bean
Phyllota phylicoides (Sieber ex DC.) Benth.	false parrot pea
Platylobium formosum Sm.	handsome flat pea
Pultenaea euchila DC.	large flower bush pea
Pultenaea rarifolia de Kok.	hairy bush pea
Pultenaea robusta (H.B.Will.) de Kok.	bush pea
Pultenaea villosa Willd.	kerosene bush
Sesbania cannabina (Retz.) Poir. var. *cannabina*	yellow pea bush
Stylosanthes humilis Kunth	Townsville stylo
Tephrosia filipes Benth. subsp. *filipes*	
Vigna luteola (Jacq.) Benth.	Dalrymple vigna
Vigna marina (Burm.) Merr.	beach vigna
Zornia dyctiocarpa DC. var. *dyctiocarpa*	
FLACOURTACEAE	
Scolopia braunii (Klotzsch) Sleumer	brown birch
FLAGELLARIACEAE	
Flagellaria indica L.	whip vine
GENTIANACEAE	
Schenkia australis (R.Br.) G.Mans.	spike centaury
GLEICHENIACEAE	
Dicranopteris linearis (Burm. f.) Underw. var. *linearis*	
Gleichenia dicarpa R.Br.	pouched coral fern
Gleichenia mendellii (G.Schneid.) S.B.Andrews	scrambling coral fern
Sticherus flabellatus (R.Br.) H.St.John var. *flabellatus*	umbrella tree fern
Sticherus lobatus N.A.Wakef.	spreading tree fern

STATUS	STRAND								
	LITTORAL FLAT								
	FORE DUNE								
	HIND DUNE								
	HIGH DUNE								
STATUS	GRASS LAND	SEDGE LAND	HERB LAND	LOW WOOD LAND	LOW OPEN FOREST	HEATH	WOOD LAND	OPEN FOREST	CLOSED FOREST
*				H			H		
*				V			V		
								V	V
						S			
									V
					S		S	S	
					S				
					S				
					S				
					S				
					S				
		H						H	
					H				
					H				
*			H						
				H	H		H	H	
				H			H		
					S		S	S	
								V	V
			H						
							H	H	
						H	H	H	
							H	H	
								H	H
								H	H

100

BOTANICAL NAME	COMMON NAME
GOODENIACEAE	
Dampiera stricta (Sm.) R.Br.	fan flower
Dampiera sylvestris Rajput & Carolin	blue dampiera
Goodenia rotundifolia R.Br.	round-leaf goodenia
Goodenia stelligera R.Br.	goodenia
Scaevola calendulacea (P.B.Kenn.) Druce	dune fan flower
Velleia spathulata R.Br.	wild pansies
HALORAGACEAE	
Gonocarpus micranthus subsp. *ramosissimus* Orchard	raspwort
Myriophyllum implicatum Orchard	water milfoil
HEMEROCALLIDACEAE	
Dianella caerulea var. *protensa* R.J.F.Hend.	blue flax lily
Dianella caerulea var. *vannata* R.J.F.Hend	blue flax lily
Dianella congesta R.Br.	blueberry lilly
Dianella crinoides R.J.F.Hend	flax lilly
Dianella longifolia R.Br.	pale flax lilly
Geitonoplesium cymosum (R.Br.) A.Cunn. ex Hook.	scrambling berry
HEMODORACEAE	
Haemodorum tenuifolium A.Cunn. ex Benth.	bloodroot
HYDROCHARITACEAE	
Vallisneria nana R.Br.	ribbonweed
HYMENOPHYLLACEAE	
Abrodictyum brassii Croxall	
Abrodictyum caudatum (Brack.) Copel.	jungle bristle fern
Abrodictyum elongatum (A. Cunn.) Copel.	
Abrodictyum obscurum (Blume) Ebihara & K.Iwats	
Crepidomanes saxifragoides (C.Presl) P.S.Green	
IRIDACEAE	
Patersonia glabrata R.Br.	bush iris

STATUS	GRASS LAND	SEDGE LAND	HERB LAND	LOW WOOD LAND	LOW OPEN FOREST	HEATH	WOOD LAND	OPEN FOREST	CLOSED FOREST
								S	
								S	
			H					H	
			H					H	
			H						
			H						
				H			H	H	
		AH							
			H				H	H	
			H						
			H				H	H	
			H						
			H						
								V	V
		H							
		H							
									E
									E
									E
									E
									H
				RH			RH	RH	

102

BOTANICAL NAME	COMMON NAME
Patersonia sericea R.Br. var. *sericea*	native iris
Sisyrinchium rosulatum E.P.Bicknell	blue-eyed grass
JOHNSONIACEAE	
Tricoryne elatior R.Br.	yellow rush lilly
Tricoryne muricata Baker	rush lilly
JUNCACEAE	
Juncus continuus L.A.S.Johnson	rush
Juncus kraussii Hochst.	sea rush
JUNCAGINACEAE	
Cycnogeton procerus (R.Br.) Mering & Kadereit	water-ribbons
Triglochin striata Ruiz & Pav.	streaked arrowgrass
LAMIACEAE	
Chloanthes parviflora Walp.	small chloanthes
Clerodendrum floribundum R.Br.	smooth clerodendrum
Gmelina leichhardtii (F.Muell.) F.Muell. ex Benth.	white beech
Plectranthus parviflorus Willd.	cockspur flower
Vitex trifolia L. var. *trifolia* L.	vitex
LAURACEAE	
Beilschmiedia elliptica C.T.White & W.D.Francis	brown walnut
Beilschmiedia obtusifolia (F.Muell. ex Meisn.) F.Muell.	hard bolly gum
Cassytha filiformis L.	dodder laurel
Cassytha glabella R.Br. forma glabella	dodder
Cassytha muelleri Meisn.	dodder
Cassytha paniculata R.Br.	dodder
Cassytha pubescens R.Br.	downy devil's vine
Cinnamomum baileyanum (F.Muell. ex F.M.Bailey) W.D.Francis	candlewood
Cinnamomum oliveri F.M.Bailey	Oliver's sassafras
Cryptocarya foetida R.T.Baker	stinking cryptocarya
Cryptocarya glaucescens R.Br.	jackwood

| STATUS | STRAND | LITTORAL FLAT | FORE DUNE | HIND DUNE | HIGH DUNE | | | | |
	GRASS LAND	SEDGE LAND	HERB LAND	LOW WOOD LAND	LOW OPEN FOREST	HEATH	WOOD LAND	OPEN FOREST	CLOSED FOREST
				RH			RH	RH	
*				H					
						H	H	H	
						H	H	H	
			H	H					
			H	H					
		AH						AH	
		AH							
			H						
				S	S		S		
									T
								S	
				T					
								T	T
								T	T
						PV	PV	PV	
						PV	PV	PV	
						PV	PV	PV	
						PV	PV	PV	
						PV	PV	PV	
E								T	T
									T
								T	
								T	T

104

BOTANICAL NAME	COMMON NAME
Cryptocarya macdonaldii B.Hyland	Mcdonald's laurel
Endiandra discolor Benth.	domatia tree
Endiandra sieberi Nees	hard corkwood
Litsea australis B.Hyland	brown bolly gum
Litsea reticulata (Meisn.) F.Muell.	bolly gum
Neolitsea dealbata (R.Br.) Merr.	white bolly gum
Persea americana Mill.	avocado
LAXMANNIACEAE	
Cordyline rubra Otto & A.Dietr.	cordyline
Cordyline terminalis (L.) Kunth	broad-leafed lilly
Eustrephus latifolius R.Br. ex Ker Gawl.	wombat berry
Laxmannia compacta Conran & P.I.Forst.	
Laxmannia gracilis R.Br.	slender wire lilly
Lomandra confertifolia subsp. *pallida* A.T.Lee	mat rush
Lomandra elongata (Benth.) Ewart	wallum mat rush
Lomandra filiformis subsp. *filiformis* (Thunb.) Britten	fine-leafed mat rush
Lomandra laxa (R.Br.) A.T.Lee	mat rush
Lomandra longifolia Labill.	common lomandra
Lomandra multiflora (R.Br.) Britten subsp. *multiflora*	many-flowered mat rush
Sowerbaea juncea Andrews	vanilla lilly
Thysanotus tuberosus R.Br. subsp. *tuberosus*	fringed lilly
LECYTHIDACEAE	
Planchonia careya (F.Muell.) R. Knuth	cocky apple
LENTIBULARIACEAE	
Utricularia bifida L.	
Utricularia biloba R.Br.	moth bladderwort
Utricularia caerulea L.	blue bladderwort
Utricularia gibba L.	floating bladderwort
Utricularia lateriflora R.Br.	small bladderwort

| STATUS | STRAND | LITTORAL FLAT | FORE DUNE | HIND DUNE | HIGH DUNE | | | | |
	GRASS LAND	SEDGE LAND	HERB LAND	LOW WOOD LAND	LOW OPEN FOREST	HEATH	WOOD LAND	OPEN FOREST	CLOSED FOREST
									T
								T	T
								T	
								T	T
									T
								T	
*								T	
								S	S
									S
				V				V	V
			H			H	H	H	
			H			H	H	H	
			TH	TH			TH	TH	TH
								TH	
							TH	TH	
					TH			TH	
				TH			TH	TH	
				TH			TH		
		H							
		H						H	
					T			T	
		H							
		H							
		H							
		H							
		H							

BOTANICAL NAME	COMMON NAME
Utricularia uliginosa Vahl	Asian bladderwort
LINDSAEACEAE	
Lindsaea brachypoda (Baker) Salomon	
Lindsaea ensifolia subsp. *agati* (Brack.) K.U.Kramer	
Lindsaea ensifolia subsp. *ensifolia* Sw.	
Lindsaea incisa Prent.	
Lindsaea repens (Bory) Thwaites	
Lindsaea repens var. *marquesensis* E.D.Br.	
LOGANIACEAE	
Mitrasacme paludosa R.Br.	sweet mitrewort
Mitrasacme polymorpha R.Br.	varied mitrewort
LOMARIOPSIDACEAE	
Nephrolepis cordifolia (L.) C.Presl.	fishbone fern
LORANTHACEAE	
Amyema bifurcata (Benth.) Tiegh.	mistletoe
Amyema cambagei (Blakely) Danser	mistletoe
Amyema congener (Sieber ex Schult. & Schult.f.) Tiegh.	erect mistletoe
Amyema mackayensis (Blakely) Danser	mistletoe
Amyema miquelii (Lehm. ex Miq.) Tiegh.	box mistletoe
Amylotheca dictyophleba (F.Muell.) Tiegh.	red mistletoe
Dendrophthoe glabrescens (Blakely) Barlow	long-flowered mistletoe
Muellerina bidwillii (Benth.) Barlow	cypress mistletoe
Muellerina celastroides (Sieber ex Schult. & Schult.f.) Tiegh.	golden mistletoe
LYCOPODIACEAE	
Lycopodiella cernua (L.) Pic.Serm	coral fern
Lycopodiella lateralis (R.Br.) B.Oilg.	slender clubmoss
Lycopodiella serpentina (Kunze) B.Oilg.	club bogmoss
LYTHRACEAE	
Cuphea carthagenensis (Jacq.) J.F.Macbr.	Columbian waxweed

107

| | | STRAND | | LITTORAL FLAT / FORE DUNE / HIND DUNE / HIGH DUNE | | | | | |
STATUS	GRASS LAND	SEDGE LAND	HERB LAND	LOW WOOD LAND	LOW OPEN FOREST	HEATH	WOOD LAND	OPEN FOREST	CLOSED FOREST
		H							
								H	H
								H	H
								H	H
									H
								H	H
								H	H
				H		H	H		
						H	H		
								H	H
			PS				PS	PS	
			PS				PS	PS	
			PS				PS	PS	
			PS						
			PS				PS	PS	
			PS				PS	PS	
			PS				PS	PS	
							PS		
					PS		PS	PS	
						H		H	H
		H				H			H
						H			H
*			H	H					

BOTANICAL NAME	COMMON NAME
MALVACEAE	
Hibiscus diversifolius Jacq. subsp. *diversifolius*	swamp hibiscus
Hibiscus tiliaceus L.	cotton tree
Sida cordifolia L.	flannelweed
Sida rhombifolia L.	sida-retusa
MARATTIACEAE	
Angiopteris evecta (G.Forst.) Hoffm.	giant fern
MELASTOMATACEAE	
Melastoma malabathricum L. subsp. *malabathricum*	blue tongue
MELIACEAE	
Dysoxylum rufum (A.Rich.) Benth.	hairy rosewood
Melia azedarach L.	white cedar
Synoum glandulosum subsp. *glandulosum* (Sm.) A.Juss.	scentless rosewood
Toona ciliata M.Roem.	red cedar
Xylocarpus granatum K.D.Koenig	cannonball mangrove
MENISPERMACEAE	
Hypserpa decumbens (Benth.) Diels	
Sarcopetalum harveyanum F.Muell.	heart-leaf vine
Stephania japonica var. *discolor* (Blume) Forman	tape vine
MENYANTHACEAE	
Nymphoides exiliflora (F.Muell.) Kuntze	marsh wort
Ornduffia reniformis (R.Br.) Tippery & Les	runing marsh flower
MIMOSACEAE	
Acacia baueri Benth. subsp. *baueri*	tiny wattle
Acacia complanata A.Cunn. ex Benth.	flat-stemmed wattle
Acacia concurrens Pedley	curracabah
Acacia disparrima M.W.McDonald & Maslin	hickory wattle
Acacia disparrima M.W.McDonald & Maslin subsp. *disparrima*	southern salwood
Acacia falcata Willd.	sickle wattle

STATUS	STRAND GRASS LAND	LITTORAL FLAT SEDGE LAND	FORE DUNE HERB LAND	HIND DUNE LOW WOOD LAND	HIGH DUNE LOW OPEN FOREST	HEATH	WOOD LAND	OPEN FOREST	CLOSED FOREST
				S	S				
				T	T				
*			H		H		H		
*			H		H		H		
									H
					S	S	S		
								T	T
									T
									T
									T
				T					
								V	V
				V	V				
				V	V				
		H							
		H							
E						S	S	S	
						T	T	T	
					T		T	T	
			T	T	T		T	T	
					S		S	S	
						S	S	S	

110

BOTANICAL NAME	COMMON NAME
Acacia falciformis DC.	broad-leaved hickory
Acacia fimbriata A.Cunn. ex G.Don	fringed wattle
Acacia flavescens A.Cunn. ex Benth.	toothed wattle
Acacia leiocalyx subsp. *herveyensis* Pedley	black wattle
Acacia leiocalyx (Domin) Pedley subsp. *leiocalyx*	black wattle
Acacia penninervis var. *longiracemosa* Domin	hickory wattle
Acacia quadrilateralis DC.	wattle
Acacia sophorae (Labill.) R.Br.	beach wattle
Acacia suaveolens (Sm.) Willd.	sweet wattle
Acacia ulicifolia (Salisb.) Court	prickly moses
Archidendron lovelliae (F.M.Bailey) I.C.Nielsen	baconwood
MOLLUGINACEAE	
Macarthuria neocambrica F.Muell.	
MONIMIACEAE	
Wilkiea huegeliana (Tul.) A.DC.	veiny wilkiea
Wilkiea macrophylla (A.Cunn.) A.DC.	large-leaved wilkiea
MORACEAE	
Ficus fraseri Miq.	white sandpaper fig
Ficus obliqua G.Forst.	small-leaved fig
Ficus opposita Miq.	sandpaper fig
Ficus rubiginosa Desf. ex Vent. forma *glabrescens*	small-leaved Moreton Bay fig
Ficus watkinsiana F.M.Bailey	strangler fig
Trophis scandens (Lour.) Hook. & Arn. subsp. *scandens*	burney vine
MYRSINACEAE	
Aegiceras corniculatum (L.) Blanco	river mangrove
Embelia australiana (F.Muell.) F.M.Bailey	embelia
Lysimachia arvensis (L.) U.Manns & Anderb.	blue pimpernel
Myrsine arenaria Jackes	northern buttonwood

STATUS	GRASS LAND	SEDGE LAND	HERB LAND	LOW WOOD LAND	LOW OPEN FOREST	HEATH	WOOD LAND	OPEN FOREST	CLOSED FOREST
							T	T	
						S			
					T		T	T	
				T	T		T		
					T		T	T	
					T		T	T	
						S			
		S	S	S					
					S	S	S		
					S	S	S		
E							T	T	
		H	H						
									S
									S
								T	T
								T	T
								S	S
								T	T
									T
					V			V	
				S					
								S	S
*					S				
					S				

BOTANICAL NAME	COMMON NAME
Myrsine subsessilis F.Muell. subsp. *subsessilis*	red buttonwood
Myrsine variabilis R.Br.	rapania
MYRTACEAE	
Acmena hemilampra (F.Muell. ex F.M.Bailey) Merr. & L.M.Perry subsp. *hemilampra*	broad-leaved lilly pilly
Acmena smithii (Poir.) Merr. & L.M.Perry	lillypilly satinash
Angophora leiocarpa (L.A.S.Johnson ex G.J.Leach) K.R.Thiele & Ladiges	smooth-barked apple
Austromyrtus dulcis (C.T.White) L.S.Sm.	midgen berry
Backhousia citriodora F.Muell.	lemon ironwood
Backhousia myrtifolia Hook. & Harv.	carrol
Baeckea frutescens L.	weeping myrtle
Baeckea linifolia Rudge	straggly baeckea
Corymbia gummifera (Gaertn.) K.D.Hill & L.A.S.Johnson	red bloodwood
Corymbia intermedia (R.T.Baker) K.D.Hill & L.A.S.Johnson	pink bloodwood
Corymbia tessellaris (F.Muell.) K.D.Hill & L.A.S. Johnson	Moreton Bay ash
Decaspermum humile (G.Don) A.J.Scott	brown myrtle
Eucalyptus grandis W.Hill	flooded gum
Eucalyptus hallii Brooker	goodwood gum
Eucalyptus latisinensis K.D.Hill	yellow stringybark
Eucalyptus microcorys F.Muell.	tallowwood
Eucalyptus pilularis Sm.	blackbutt
Eucalyptus planchoniana F.Muell.	needlebark stringybark
Eucalyptus racemosa Cav. subsp. *racemosa* Sm.	scribbly gum
Eucalyptus resinifera Sm.	red mahogany
Eucalyptus robusta Sm.	swamp mahogany
Eucalyptus robusta x *E. tereticornis* Sm.	
Eucalyptus siderophloia Benth.	grey ironbark
Eucalyptus tereticornis Sm.	forest red gum

STATUS	GRASS LAND	SEDGE LAND	HERB LAND	LOW WOOD LAND	LOW OPEN FOREST	HEATH	WOOD LAND	OPEN FOREST	CLOSED FOREST
							S	S	
					S		S	S	
									T
								T	T
					T		T		
					S	S	S	S	
								T	T
								T	T
							S	S	
							S	S	
					T		T	T	
					T		T	T	
					T				
								S	
*								T	
				T	T				
				T		T			
								T	
							T	T	
						T			
					T	T	T		
							T	T	
						T			
						T	T		
					T				
					T		T		

114

BOTANICAL NAME	COMMON NAME
Homoranthus virgatus A.Cunn. ex Schauer	twiggy homoranthus
Leptospermum juniperinum Sm.	prickly tea-tree
Leptospermum liversidgei R.T.Baker & H.G.Sm.	swamp may
Leptospermum petersonii F.M.Bailey	lemon scented tea tree
Leptospermum polygalifolium Salisb.	yellow tea-tree
Leptospermum semibaccatum Cheel	wallum tea-tree
Leptospermum speciosum Schauer	wild may
Leptospermum trinervium (Sm.) Joy Thomps.	wooly tea-tree
Lophostemon confertus (R.Br.) Peter G.Wilson & J.T.Waterh.	brush box
Lophostemon suaveolens (Sol. ex Gaertn.) Peter G.Wilson & J.T.Waterh.	swamp box
Melaleuca dealbata S.T.Blake	swamp tee tree
Melaleuca nodosa (Gaertn.) Sm.	prickly paperbark
Melaleuca pachyphylla (Cheel) Craven	wallum bottlebrush
Melaleuca quinquenervia (Cav.) S.T.Blake	swamp paperbark
Ochrosperma lineare (C.T.White) Trudgen	straggly baeckea
Osbornia octodonta F.Muell.	myrtle mangrove
Pilidiostigma glabrum Burret	plum myrtle
Rhodamnia acuminata C.T.White	Cooloola ironwood
Rhodamnia dumicola Guymer & Jessup	whire myrtle
Sannantha bidwillii (A.R.Bean) Peter G.Wilson	tall baeckea
Syncarpia hillii F.M.Bailey	Fraser Island satinay
Syzygium australe (H.L.Wendl. ex Link) B.Hyland	scrub cherry
Syzygium johnsonii (F.Muell.) B.Hyland	Johnson's satinash
Syzygium luehmannii (F.Muell.) L.A.S.Johnson	small-leaved lilly pilly
Syzygium oleosum (F.Muell.) B.Hyland	blue lilly pilly
NYMPHAECEAE	
Nymphaea caerulea Savigny	South African waterlilly

| STATUS | STRAND | | | LITTORAL FLAT | FORE DUNE | HIND DUNE | HIGH DUNE | | |
	GRASS LAND	SEDGE LAND	HERB LAND	LOW WOOD LAND	LOW OPEN FOREST	HEATH	WOOD LAND	OPEN FOREST	CLOSED FOREST
					S		S	S	
						S	S		
						S	S		
								S	
						S	S	S	
						S	S	S	
							S	S	
							S	S	
				T	T		T	T	T
							T		
					S	S			
					S				
				S	S	S			
					T		T		
							S	S	
				T					
								S	S
								T	T
								T	T
							S	S	
E								T	T
								T	T
								T	T
									T
									T
*		H							

116

BOTANICAL NAME	COMMON NAME
OLEACEAE	
Notelaea longifolia Vent. forma *glabra* P.S.Green	large mock-olive
Notelaea punctata R.Br.	forest olive
Olax retusa Benth.	olax
ONAGRACEAE	
Oenothera affinis Cambess.	long-flowered primrose
Oenothera drummondii Hook. subsp. *drummondii*	beach primrose
OPHIOGLOSSACEAE	
Ophioglossum pendulum L.	ribbon fern
ORCHIDACEAE	
Acianthus exsertus R.Br.	mosquito orchid
Acianthus fornicatus R.Br.	pixie caps
Acianthus pusillus D.L.Jones	small mosquito orchid
Arthrochilus irritabilis F.Muell.	leafy elbow orchid
Bulbophyllum schillerianum Rchb.f.	red rope orchid
Caladenia alata R.Br.	fairy orchid
Caladenia carnea R.Br.	pink fingers
Caladenia catenata (Sm.) Druce	white caladenia
Caladenia fuscata (Rchb.f.) M.A.Clem. & D.L.Jones	dusky fingers
Calanthe triplicata (Willemet) Ames	Christmas orchid
Caleana major R.Br.	flying duck orchid
Calochilus grandiflorus (Benth.) Domin	copper beard orchid
Chiloglottis diphylla R.Br.	common wasp orchid
Chiloglottis sylvestris D.L. Jones & M.A. Clem.	small wasp orchid
Corunastylis acuminata (R.S.Rogers) D.L.Jones & M.A.Clem	
Corybas undulatus (R. Cunn.) Rupp	tailed helmut orchid
Cryptostylis erecta R.Br.	bonnet orchid
Cymbidium madidum Lindl.	arrowroot orchid
Cymbidium suave R.Br.	snake flower

| | | | | STRAND | LITTORAL FLAT | FORE DUNE | HIND DUNE | HIGH DUNE | |
STATUS	GRASS LAND	SEDGE LAND	HERB LAND	LOW WOOD LAND	LOW OPEN FOREST	HEATH	WOOD LAND	OPEN FOREST	CLOSED FOREST
								T	T
								T	T
						H	H	H	
*			H						
*			H						
									E
							H		
							H		
				E	E				
							H		
							H	H	
							H	H	
							H	H	
							H	H	
							H	H	
								H	H
						H	H		
								H	
							H		
							H		
				H	H				
							H		
							H		
							E	E	
							E	E	

BOTANICAL NAME	COMMON NAME
Dendrobium aemulum R.Br.	ironbark orchid
Dendrobium gracilicaule F.Muell.	slender orchid
Dendrobium speciosum F.Muell.	king orchid
Dendrobium tetragonum A.Cunn.	spider orchid
Dipodium variegatum M.A.Clem. & D.L.Jones	hyacinth orchid
Diteilis simmondsii (F.M.Bailey) M.A.Clem. & D.L.Jones	coastal sprite orchid,
Diuris alba R.Br.	white donkey orchid
Diuris aurea Sm.	golden diuris
Dockrillia bowmanii (Benth.) M.A.Clem. & D.L.Jones	straggly pencil orchid
Dockrillia linguiformis (Sw.) Brieger	tongue orchid
Dockrillia mortii F.Muell.	mort's dockrillia
Erythrorchis cassythoides (A.Cunn.) Garay	climbing orchid
Genoplesium psammophilum D.L.Jones	
Genoplesium pumilum (Hook.f.) D.L.Jones & M.A.Clem.	green midge orchid
Genoplesium sp. (Fraser Island NP R.Crane 2063)	
Geodorum densiflorum (Lam.) Schltr.	pink nodding orchid
Glossodia minor R.Br.	small waxlip orchid
Microtis parviflora R.Br.	slender onion orchid
Oberonia complanata (A.Cunn.) M.A.Clem. & D.L.Jones	
Oberonia palmicola F.Muell.	soldiers crest orchid
Paracaleana minor (R.Br.) Blaxell	small duck orchid
Peristeranthus hillii (F.Muell.) T.E.Hunt	beetle orchid
Phaius australis F.Muell.	swamp orchid
Prasophyllum brevilabre (Lindl.) Hook.f.	short-lip leek orchid
Prasophyllum exilis D.L.Jones & R.J.Bates	wallum leek orchid
Pterostylis acuminata R.Br.	sharp greenhood
Pterostylis antennifera (D.L.Jones) D.L.Jones.	greenhood orchid
Pterostylis baptistii Fitzg.	king greenhood
Pterostylis erecta T.E.Hunt	erect maroonhood

119

| STATUS | STRAND | | | LITTORAL FLAT | FORE DUNE | HIND DUNE | HIGH DUNE | | |
	GRASS LAND	SEDGE LAND	HERB LAND	LOW WOOD LAND	LOW OPEN FOREST	HEATH	WOOD LAND	OPEN FOREST	CLOSED FOREST
									E
									E
									E
									E
				H	H		H		
E									H
						H	H		
						H	H		
								E	
									E
									E
									E
							H		
							H		
							H		
							H	H	
						H	H	H	
							H		
									E
		E							
							H	H	
								E	E
E				H	H	H			
	H								
					H		H		
								H	H
								H	H
							H	H	
								H	H

BOTANICAL NAME	COMMON NAME
Pterostylis hispidula Fitzg.	nodding greenhood
Pterostylis nigricans D.L.Jones & M.A.Clem.	dark greenhood orchid
Pterostylis nutans R.Br.	nodding greenhood orchid
Pterostylis ophioglossa R.Br.	snake tongue greenhood
Pterostylis parviflora R.Br.	tiny greenhood
Pterostylis revoluta R.Br.	autumn green orchid
Rhinerrhiza divitiflora (F.Muell. ex Benth.) Rupp	raspy root orchid
Taeniophyllum muelleri Lindl. ex Benth.	minute orchid
Thelymitra ixioides Sw.	dotted sun orchid
Thelymitra purpurata Rupp	wallum sun orchid
Zeuxine oblonga R.S.Rogers & C.T.White	hairy jewel orchid
OROBANCHACEAE	
Buchnera urticifolia R.Br.	blackrod
OSMUNDACEAE	
Todea barbara (L.) T.Moore	king fern
OXALIDACEAE	
Oxalis corniculata L.	creeping oxalis
Oxalis perennans Haw.	sorrel
Oxalis pes-caprae L.	yellow sorrel
Oxalis rubens Haw.	sorrel
PANDANACEAE	
Freycinetia scandens Gaudich.	climbing pandanus
Pandanus tectorius Parkinson ex Du Roi	long-leaved pandanus
PAPAVERACEAE	
Argemone ochroleuca Sweet subsp. *ochroleuca*	Mexican poppy
PASSIFLORACEAE	
Passiflora edulis Sims.	common passionfruit
Passiflora pallida L.	corky passion flower

121

Zone groupings (overlapping bars, left to right): STRAND · LITTORAL FLAT · FORE DUNE · HIND DUNE · HIGH DUNE

STATUS	GRASS LAND	SEDGE LAND	HERB LAND	LOW WOOD LAND	LOW OPEN FOREST	HEATH	WOOD LAND	OPEN FOREST	CLOSED FOREST
							H	H	
							H	H	
							H	H	
								H	
							H	H	
							H	H	
								H	
								E	E
						H	H	H	
						H	H	H	
									H
		H	H						
									H
			H		H		H	H	
			H		H		H	H	
*			H		H		H	H	
			H		H		H	H	
									V
	T			T					
*		H	H	H					
*							V		
*							V		

122

BOTANICAL NAME	COMMON NAME
PHILYDRACEAE	
Philydrum lanuginosum Banks & Sol. ex Gaertn.	woolly water lilly
PHYLLANTHACEAE	
Breynia oblongifolia (Muell.Arg.) Muell.Arg.	coffee bush
Glochidion ferdinandi (Muell.Arg.) F.M.Bailey	cheese tree
Glochidion lobocarpum (Benth.) F.M.Bailey	pin flower tree
Glochidion sumatranum Miq.	button wood
Phyllanthus tenellus Roxb.	hen and chicken
Phyllanthus virgatus G.Forst.	creeping phyllanthus
Poranthera microphylla Brongn.	small poranthera
PICRODENRACEAE	
Petalostigma pubescens Domin	quinine tree
Pseudanthus orientalis F.Muell.	coastal pseudanthus
PIPERACEAE	
Piper caninum Blume	pepper vine
Piper hederaceum (Miq.) A.Cunn. ex C.DC. var. *hederaceum*	giant pepper vine
PITTOSPORACEAE	
Pittosporum revolutum W.T.Aiton	hairy pittosporum
PLANTAGINACEAE	
Bacopa monnieri (L.) Pennell	herb of grace
Plantago lanceolata L.	ribwort plantain
PLUMBAGINACEAE	
Aegialitis annulata R.Br.	club mangrove
Limonium solanderi Lincz.	native sea lavender
POACEAE	
Aira cupaniana Guss	silver hair grass
Alloteropsis semialata (R.Br.) Hitchc.	cockatoo grass
Andropogon virginicus L.	whiskey grass
Aristida benthamii Henrard var. *benthamii*	wire grass

STATUS	GRASS LAND	SEDGE LAND	HERB LAND	LOW WOOD LAND	LOW OPEN FOREST	HEATH	WOOD LAND	OPEN FOREST	CLOSED FOREST
		AH							
								S	S
					T		T	T	
					T		T	T	
					T		T	T	
*			H				H	H	
			H				H	H	
			H				H		
					T		T	T	T
					S	S	S	S	
									V
									V
								S	S
		H							
*				H					
				S					
			H	H					
*				H				H	
	H		H						
*	H		H						
				TH					

BOTANICAL NAME	COMMON NAME
Aristida calycina R.Br. var. *calycina*	dark wire grass
Aristida holathera Domin var. *holathera*	wire grass
Axonopus compressus (Sw.) P.Beauv.	broad-leaf carpet grass
Axonopus fissifolius (Raddi) Kuhlm.	narrow-leaf carpet grass
Briza maxima L.	great quaking grass
Briza minor L.	little quaking grass
Bromus catharticus Vahl	prairie grass
Cenchrus echinatus L.	Mossman River grass
Chloris gayana Kunth	Rhodes grass
Chloris inflata Link	purpletop chloris
Cymbopogon refractus (R.Br.) A.Camus	barb wire grass
Cynodon dactylon (L.) Pers. var. *dactylon*	green couch
Digitaria ciliaris (Retz.) Koeler	summer grass
Digitaria didactyla Willd.	Qld blue couch
Digitaria leucostachya (Domin) Henrard	coastal dune digitaria
Digitaria parviflora (R.Br.) Hughes	small flower
Digitaria violascens Link	bastard summer grass
Diplachne fusca (L.) P.Beauv. ex Roem. & Schult. var. fusca	
Echinochloa crus-galli (L.) P.Beauv.	barnyard grass
Echinochloa telmatophila P.W.Michael & Vickery	swamp barnyard grass
Eleusine indica (L.) Gaertn.	crowsfoot grass
Elionurus citreus (R.Br.) Munro. ex Benth.	lemon-scented grass
Entolasia marginata (R.Br.) Hughes	bordered panic
Entolasia stricta (R.Br.) Hughes	wiry panic
Entolasia whiteana C.E.Hubb.	
Eragrostis brownii (Kunth) Nees ex Wight	brown's love grass
Eragrostis curvula (Schrad.) Nees	African love grass
Eragrostis elongata (Willd.) J.Jacq.	clustered love grass
Eragrostis interrupta P.Beauv.	coastal dune love grass

125

| STATUS | STRAND | LITTORAL FLAT | FORE DUNE | HIND DUNE | HIGH DUNE | | | | |
	GRASS LAND	SEDGE LAND	HERB LAND	LOW WOOD LAND	LOW OPEN FOREST	HEATH	WOOD LAND	OPEN FOREST	CLOSED FOREST
	TH			TH					
*	H		H						
*	H		H						
*								H	
*								H	
*			H						
*			H						
*			TH						
*			TH						
			TH						
*	H		H						
*			H						
			H	H					
	TH		TH						
			TH						
*			TH						
			H						
*			H						
			H						
*			H						
			H						
			H						
			H						
			H						
			H						
*			H						
			H						
			H						

BOTANICAL NAME	COMMON NAME
Eragrostis parviflora (R.Br.) Trin.	weeping love grass
Eragrostis spartinoides Steud.	love grass
Eragrostis tenuifolia (A.Rich.) Hochst. ex Steud.	elastic grass
Eremochloa bimaculata Hack.	poverty grass
Eriachne glabrata (Maiden) W.Hartley	wanderrie grass
Eriachne insularis Domin	wanderrie grass
Eriachne pallescens R.Br.	wanderrie grass
Eriachne pallescens R.Br. var. *pallescens*	wanderrie grass
Eriachne pallescens var. *gracilis* (Brongn.) Lazarides	wanderrie grass
Eriachne rara R.Br.	wanderrie grass
Eriochloa fatmensis (Hochst. & Steud.) Clayton	
Eriochloa procera (Retz.) C.E.Hubb.	early spring grass
Imperata cylindrica (L.) Raeusch.	blady grass
Ischaemum australe R.Br. var. *australe*	large blue grass
Ischaemum fragile R.Br.	
Ischaemum muticum L.	
Ischaemum triticeum R.Br.	
Leersia hexandra Sw.	swamp rice grass
Lepturus repens (G.Forst.) R.Br.	beach lepturus
Lolium rigidum Gaudin	
Melinis repens (Willd.) Zizka	red natal grass
Oplismenus aemulus (R.Br.) Roem. & Schult.	creeping shade grass
Oplismenus imbecillis (R.Br.) Roem. & Schult.	panic grass
Oplismenus mollis (Domin) Clifford & Evans ex B.K.Simon	
Panicum effusum R.Br.	hairy panic
Panicum lachnophyllum Benth.	don't panic
Panicum simile Domin	two colour panic
Paspalidium constrictum (Domin) C.E.Hubb.	knottybutt grass
Paspalidium gausum S.T.Blake	

STATUS	GRASS LAND	SEDGE LAND	HERB LAND	LOW WOOD LAND	LOW OPEN FOREST	HEATH	WOOD LAND	OPEN FOREST	CLOSED FOREST
			H						
			H						
*			H						
					H				
					TH		TH	TH	
					TH		TH	TH	
					TH		TH		
					TH		TH		
					TH		TH		
					TH		TH		
					TH		TH		
							TH	TH	
					TH		TH	TH	
				RH	RH		RH	RH	
	RH				RH		RH	RH	
	RH				RH		RH	RH	
			H						
			H						
		AH							
			H						
				H					
*			H						
					H		H	H	
					H		H	H	
					H		H	H	
					H		H	H	
					H		H	H	
							H	H	
		H	H			H			
			H						

128

BOTANICAL NAME	COMMON NAME
Paspalidium gracile (R.Br.) Hughes	slender panic
Paspalum conjugatum P.J.Bergius	sour grass
Paspalum dilatatum Poir.	
Paspalum mandiocanum Trin.	broadleaf paspalum
Paspalum scrobiculatum L.	dutch millet
Paspalum vaginatum Sw.	salt water couch
Phragmites australis (Cav.) Trin. ex Steud.	common reed
Poa annua L.	
Pseudoraphis paradoxa (R.Br.) Pilg.	slender mudgrass
Schizachyrium fragile (R.Br.) A.Camus	fire grass
Setaria sphacelata (Schumach.) Stapf & C.E.Hubb.	South African pigeon grass
Setaria surgens Stapf	
Spinifex sericeus R.Br.	beach spinefix
Sporobolus africanus (Poir.) Robyns & Tournay	Paramatta grass
Sporobolus fertilis (Steud.) Clayton	giant Paramatta grass
Sporobolus laxus B.K.Simon	rats tail grass
Sporobolus virginicus (L.) Kunth	marine couch
Stenotaphrum secundatum (Walter) Kuntze	St Augustine grass
Themeda triandra Forssk.	kangaroo grass
Urochloa decumbens (Stapf) R.D.Webster	signal grass
Urochloa distachya (L.) Nguyen	
Urochloa mutica (Forssk.) Nguyen	para grass
Vulpia bromoides (L.) Gray	hair grass
Zoysia macrantha Desv. subsp. *macrantha*	prickly couch
PODOCARPACEAE	
Podocarpus elatus R.Br. ex Endl.	brown pine
POLYGALACEAE	
Comesperma defoliatum F.Muell.	leafless milkwort
Comesperma retusum Labill.	

STATUS	GRASS LAND	SEDGE LAND	HERB LAND	LOW WOOD LAND	LOW OPEN FOREST	HEATH	WOOD LAND	OPEN FOREST	CLOSED FOREST
		H						H	
*		AH						AH	
*		AH						AH	
*		TH						TH	
					TH		TH	TH	
		AH						AH	
		AH						AH	
				H	H				
					H		H	H	
		H	H	H		H	H		
*			TH				TH	TH	
			TH				TH	TH	
	H								
*			RH	RH					
*			RH	RH					
			RH	RH					
			RH	RH					
*			RH	RH			RH		
			TH	TH	TH		TH	TH	
			H	H	H				
			H					H	
			H	H	H				
				H				H	H
			H	H	H				
									T
								S	
								S	

130

BOTANICAL NAME	COMMON NAME
POLYGONACEAE	
Acetosella vulgaris Fourr.	sheep sorrel
Persicaria orientalis (L.) Spach	princes feathers
Drynaria rigidula (Sw.) Bedd.	basket fern
Microsorum maximum (Brack.) Copel.	
Microsorum punctatum (L.) Copel.	
Microsorum scandens (G.Forst.) Tindale	fragrant climbing fern
Platycerium bifurcatum (Cav.) C.Chr.	elkhorn
Platycerium superbum de Jonch. & Hennipman	staghorn
Pyrrosia rupestris (R.Br.) Ching	rock felt fern
PORTULACEAE	
Portulaca pilosa L.	hairy pigweed
PROTACEAE	
Banksia integrifolia L.f. subsp. *compar* (R.Br.) K.R. Thiele	coastal banksia
Banksia aemula R.Br.	wallum banksia
Banksia integrifolia L.f. subsp. *integrifolia*	coastal banksia
Banksia oblongifolia Cav.	dwarf banksia
Banksia robur Cav.	broad-leaved banksia
Banksia serrata L.f.	red honeysuckle
Conospermum taxifolium C.F.Gaertn.	devils rice
Grevillea reptans Makinson	
Grevillea robusta A.Cunn. ex R.Br.	southern silky oak
Hakea actites W.R.Barker	wallum hakea
Persoonia media R.Br.	
Persoonia prostrata R.Br.	geebung
Persoonia stradbrokensis Domin	geebung
Persoonia tenuifolia R.Br.	narrow-leafed geebung
Persoonia virgata R.Br.	small-leaved geebung
Petrophile shirleyae F.M.Bailey	conesticks

| STATUS | STRAND | | | HIGH DUNE / HIND DUNE / FORE DUNE / LITTORAL FLAT | | | | | |
	GRASS LAND	SEDGE LAND	HERB LAND	LOW WOOD LAND	LOW OPEN FOREST	HEATH	WOOD LAND	OPEN FOREST	CLOSED FOREST
*			H		H		H	H	
					H				
									E
								H	H
								H	H
								H	H
									E
									E
									E
*			H	H	H				
				T	T				
		T			T	T	T	T	
				T	T				
						T	T		
				S	S	S			
					T		T		
					S	S	S		
				S					
*								T	
					S	S	S		
					S		S		
E					S		S		
					S		S		
					S		S		
					S		S	S	
					S				

132

BOTANICAL NAME	COMMON NAME
Strangea linearis Meisn.	strangea
Xylomelum benthamii Orchard	woody pear
PSILOTACEAE	
Psilotum nudum (L.) P.Beauv.	skeleton fork fern
Tmesipteris truncata (R.Br.) Desv.	
PTERIDACEAE	
Adiantum hispidulum Sw.	rough maidenhair fern
Adiantum hispidulum var. *hypoglaucum* Domin	maidenhair fern
Haplopteris ensiformis (Sw.) E.H.Crane	tape fern
Pityrogramma calomelanos var. *austroamericana* (Domin) Farw.	golden fern
Pteris comans G.Forst.	netted bracken
RANUNCULACEAE	
Clematis glycinoides DC.	forest clematis
Clematis pickeringii A. Gray	tropical clematis
RESTIONACEAE	
Baloskion pallens (R.Br.) B.G.Briggs & L.A.S.Johnson	cord rush
Baloskion tenuiculme (S.T.Blake) B.G.Biggs & L.A.S. Johnson	cord-rush
Baloskion tetraphyllum subsp. *meiostachyum* (L.A.S.Johnson & O.D.Evans) B.G.Briggs & L.A.S.Johnson	feather plant
Coleocarya gracilis S.T.Blake	sedge
Empodisma minus (Hook.f.) L.A.S.Johnson & D.F.Cutler	spreading rope rush
Hypolaena fastigiata R.Br.	tassle rope rush
Leptocarpus tenax (Labill.) R.Br.	
*Sporadanthus caudata (*L.A.S.Johnson & O.D. Evans) B.G. Briggs & L.A.S. Johnson	
Sporadanthus interruptus (F.Muell.) B.G.Briggs & L.A.S.Johnson	
RHAMNACEAE	
Alphitonia excelsa (Fenzl) Benth.	red ash
Alphitonia petriei Braid & C.T.White	pink ash

133

STATUS	GRASS LAND	SEDGE LAND	HERB LAND	LOW WOOD LAND	LOW OPEN FOREST	HEATH	WOOD LAND	OPEN FOREST	CLOSED FOREST
						S			
				T	T		T		
									H
									E
								H	
								H	
									E
								H	H
									H
								V	V
								V	V
		H	H						
		H							
		H	H						
		H							
		H							
		H							
		H							
		H							
		H							
				T	T		T		
								T	T

STRAND · **LITTORAL FLAT** · **FORE DUNE** · **HIND DUNE** · **HIGH DUNE**

BOTANICAL NAME	COMMON NAME
Emmenosperma alphitonioides F.Muell.	grey ash
Emmenosperma cunninghamii Benth.	yellow ash
RHIZOPHORACEAE	
Bruguiera gymnorhiza (L.) Savigny	orange mangrove
Ceriops australis (C.T.White) Ballment, T.J.Sm. & J.A.Stoddart	yellow mangrove
Rhizophora mucronata Lam.	
Rhizophora stylosa Griff.	spotted leaved red mangrove
RIPOGONACEAE	
Ripogonum discolor F.Muell.	prickly supplejack
RUBIACEAE	
Atractocarpus chartaceus (F.Muell.) Puttock	narrow-leafed gardenia
Coelospermum paniculatum F.Muell. var. *paniculatum*	medicine bush
Cyclophyllum coprosmoides var. *spathulatum* (O.Schwarz) S.T.Reynolds & R.J.F.Hend.	
Cyclophyllum longipetalum S.T.Reynolds & R.J.F.Hend.	
Gynochthodes canthoides F.Muell.	veiny morinda
Gynochthodes jasminoides (A.Cunn.) Razafim. & B.Bremer	morinda
Gynochthodes umbellata (L.) Razafim. & B.Bremer	morinda
Pomax umbellata (Gaertn.) Sol. ex A.Rich.	dwarf's umbrella
Psychotria daphnoides A.Cunn.	smooth psychotria
Psychotria loniceroides Sieber ex DC.	hairy psychotria
Psydrax lamprophylla (F.Muell.) Bridson forma *lamprophylla*	sweet susie
Richardia brasiliensis Gomes	white eye
Spermacoce brachystema R.Br. ex Benth.	
Spermacoce multicaulis Benth	
Timonius timon (Spreng.) Merr. var. timon	timonius
RUTACEAE	
Acronychia imperforata F.Muell.	beach acronychia

| STATUS | STRAND | | | LITTORAL FLAT | FORE DUNE | HIND DUNE | HIGH DUNE | | |
	GRASS LAND	SEDGE LAND	HERB LAND	LOW WOOD LAND	LOW OPEN FOREST	HEATH	WOOD LAND	OPEN FOREST	CLOSED FOREST
								T	T
								T	T
				T					
				S					
				S					
				S					
									V
									S
									V
				T	T			T	
				T	T			T	
							V	V	
							V	V	
							V	V	
					H		H	H	
					S		S	S	
				S	S		S	S	
					T		T	T	
*					H		H		
			H		H				
			H						
				T	T				
				T	T			T	

BOTANICAL NAME	COMMON NAME
Acronychia laevis J.R.Forst. & G.Forst.	glossy acronychia
Acronychia pubescens (F.M.Bailey) C.T.White	hairy acronychia
Acronychia wilcoxiana (F.Muell.) T.G.Hartley	silver aspen
Boronia bipinnata Lindl.	rock boronia
Boronia falcifolia A.Cunn. ex Endl.	wallum boronia
Boronia occidentalis Duretto	boronia
Boronia parviflora Sm.	swamp boronia
Boronia rivularis C.T.White	Wide Bay boronia
Boronia rosmarinifolia A.Cunn. ex Endl.	forest boronia
Citrus x limon (L.) Osbeck	bush lemon
Eriostemon australasius Pers.	pink wax flower
Flindersia bennettii F.Muell. & C.Moore	Bennet's ash
Flindersia schottiana F.Muell.	bumpy ash
Halfordia kendack (Montrouz.) Guillaumin	safron heart
Medicosma cunninghamii (Hook.) Hook.f.	pink heart
Melicope elleryana (F.Muell.) T.G.Hartley	pink flowered evodia
Melicope vitiflora (F.Muell.) T.G.Hartley	northern evodia
Phebalium woombye (F.M.Bailey) Domin	wallum woombye
Pitaviaster haplophyllus (F.Muell.) T.G.Hartley	yellow aspen
Sarcomelicope simplicifolia (Endl.) T.G.Hartley subsp. *simplicifolia*	yellow aspen
Zieria laxiflora (Benth.) Domin	wallum zieria
Zieria smithii Jacks.	lanoline-bush
SANTALACEAE	
Choretrum candollei F.Muell. ex Benth.	white sour bush
Exocarpos cupressiformis Labill.	native cherry
Leptomeria acida R.Br.	sour current bush
SAPINDACEAE	
Alectryon reticulatus Radlk.	wild quince

Zone groupings (stepped headers, left to right): STRAND · LITTORAL FLAT · FORE DUNE · HIND DUNE · HIGH DUNE

STATUS	GRASS LAND	SEDGE LAND	HERB LAND	LOW WOOD LAND	LOW OPEN FOREST	HEATH	WOOD LAND	OPEN FOREST	CLOSED FOREST
				T	T		T	T	
							T	T	
								T	T
							S	S	
					S				
					S		S		
					S				
E					S		S		
							S	S	
*				S	S		S		
				S	S		S		
									T
									T
								T	T
									S
							T	T	
									T
					S		S	S	
									T
								T	T
				S	S		S	S	
				S	S		S	S	
					S			S	
					PS		PS	PS	
					S		S	S	
								T	T

BOTANICAL NAME	COMMON NAME
Cupaniopsis anacardioides (A.Rich.) Radlk.	tuckeroo
Dodonaea triquetra J.C.Wendl.	large-leaved hop bush
Dodonaea viscosa subsp. *burmanniana* (DC.) J.G.West	sticky hop bush
Dodonaea viscosa subsp. *viscosa* Jacq	
Elattostachys nervosa (F.Muell.) Radlk.	green tamarind
Guioa acutifolia Radlk.	northern guioa
Harpullia alata F.Muell.	winged-leaved tulipwood
Harpullia pendula Planch. ex F.Muell.	tulipwood
Jagera pseudorhus (A.Rich.) Radlk. var. *pseudorhus*	foam bark tree
Mischarytera lautereriana (F.M.Bailey) H.Turner	corduroy tamarind
Mischocarpus australis S.T.Reynolds	red pear fruit
Mischocarpus pyriformis (F.Muell.) Radlk. subsp. *pyriformis*	yellow pear fruit
Sarcopteryx stipata (F.Muell.) Radlk.	steelwood
Toechima tenax (A.Cunn. ex Benth.) Radlk.	pitted-leaf steelwood
SAPOTACEAE	
Planchonella australis (R.Br.) Pierre	black apple
Planchonella chartacea (F.Muell. ex Benth.) H.J.Lam	thin-leaved coondoo
Pleioluma queenslandica (P. Royan) Swenson	bush coondoo
SCHIZAEACEAE	
Lygodium microphyllum (Cav.) R.Br.	snake fern
Schizaea bifida Willd.	comb fern
SCROPHULARIACEAE	
Artanema fimbricatum D.Don	
Myoporum acuminatum R.Br.	coastal boobiala
Myoporum boninense subsp. *australe* Chinnock	chinnock
Scoparia dulcis L.	bitter broom
SELAGINELLACEAE	
Selaginella uliginosa (Labill.) Spring	swamp selaginella

STATUS	STRAND	LITTORAL FLAT	FORE DUNE	HIND DUNE	HIGH DUNE				
	GRASS LAND	SEDGE LAND	HERB LAND	LOW WOOD LAND	LOW OPEN FOREST	HEATH	WOOD LAND	OPEN FOREST	CLOSED FOREST
				T	T				
			S	S	S		S	S	
					S		S	S	
					S		S	S	
									T
								T	T
									T
									T
				T	T				
								T	T
									T
									T
									T
									T
					T		T	T	
								T	T
								T	T
			H	H	H		H	H	H
							H	H	H
		.	H	H					
			S		S				
			S		S				
			H		H				
		H				H			

140

BOTANICAL NAME	COMMON NAME
SIMAROUBACEAE	
Ailanthus triphysa (Dennst.) Alston	white siris
SMILACACEAE	
Smilax australis R.Br.	barb wire vine
Smilax glyciphylla Sm.	sasparilla vine
SOLANACEAE	
Duboisia myoporoides R.Br.	poisonous corkwood
Solanum nigrum L. subsp. *nigrum*	blackberry nightshade
Solanum nodiflorum Jacq.	glossy nightshade
STACKHOUSIACEAE	
Stackhousia spathulata Sieber ex Spreng.	coast stackhousia
Stackhousia viminea Sm.	slender stackhousia
STERCULIACEAE	
Brachychiton populneus (Schott & Endl.) R.Br. subsp. *populneus*	kurrajong
STYLIDIACEAE	
Stylidium graminifolium Sw.	grass-trigger plant
Stylidium ornatum S.T.Blake	trigger plant
Stylidium tenerum Spreng.	trigger plant
SYMPLOCACEAE	
Symplocos stawellii F.Muell.	white hazelwood
TECTARIACEAE	
Arthropteris tenella (G. Forst.) J.Sm.ex Hook. f.C.Presl	climbing fishbone fern
THELYPTERIDACEAE	
Christella dentata (Forssk.) Brownsey & Jermy	water fern
THYMELAEACEAE	
Phaleria chermsideana (F.M.Bailey) C.T.White	scrub daphne
Phaleria octandra (L.) Baill	phaleria
Pimelea linifolia Sm.	queen of the bush
Pimelea linifolia Sm. subsp. *linifolia*	rice flower

| | STRAND | | | LITTORAL FLAT | FORE DUNE | HIND DUNE | HIGH DUNE | | |
STATUS	GRASS LAND	SEDGE LAND	HERB LAND	LOW WOOD LAND	LOW OPEN FOREST	HEATH	WOOD LAND	OPEN FOREST	CLOSED FOREST
									T
							V	V	V
							V	V	V
								T	T
			S						
*			H						
	H	H							
	H	H	H						
								T	
						H	H		
						H			
						H			
								T	T
								H	H
								H	H
								T	T
								S	S
					S		S	S	
					S		S	S	

142

BOTANICAL NAME	COMMON NAME
Wikstroemia indica (L.) C.A.Mey.	
ULMACEAE	
Celtis paniculata (Endl.) Planch.	native celtis
Trema tomentosa var. *aspera* (Brongn.) Hewson	poison peach
VERBENACEAE	
Lantana camara L.	lantana
Phyla nodiflora (L.) Greene	frog fruit
Verbena rigida f. lilacina 'Polaris'	slender vervain
VIOLACEAE	
Hybanthus monopetalus (Schult.) Domin	ladies slipper
Hybanthus stellariodes (Domin) P.I.Forst.	ladies slipper
Viola hederacea Labill.	native violet
Notothixos subaureus Oliv.	golden mistletoe
VISCACEAE	
Viscum articulatum Burm.f.	flat mistletoe
VITACEAE	
Cissus hypoglauca A.Gray	five-leaved water vine
Cissus sterculiifolia (F.Muell. ex Benth.) Planch.	long -leaf water vine
Clematicissus opaca (F.Muell.) Jackes & Rossetto	yam
WINTERACEAE	
Tasmannia insipida R.Br.	brush pepperbush
XANTHORRHOEACEAE	
Xanthorrhoea fulva (A.T.Lee) D.J.Bedford	swamp grass tree
Xanthorrhoea johnsonii A.T.Lee	forest grass tree
Xanthorrhoea macronema F.Muell. ex Benth.	grass tree
XYRIDACEAE	
Xyris complanata R.Br.	yellow eye
Xyris juncea R.Br.	hatpins
Xyris operculata Labill.	

| STATUS | STRAND | LITTORAL FLAT | FORE DUNE | HIND DUNE | HIGH DUNE | | | | |
	GRASS LAND	SEDGE LAND	HERB LAND	LOW WOOD LAND	LOW OPEN FOREST	HEATH	WOOD LAND	OPEN FOREST	CLOSED FOREST
	S								
				S	S		S		
				S	S		S		
*				S	S				
			H		H		H	H	
			H						
					H		H	H	
					H		H	H	
					H	H	H	H	
					PS		PS	PS	
				PS	PS		PS	PS	
				V	V		V	V	V
				V	V		V	V	V
				V	V		V	V	V
									S
						S	S	S	
					S		S		
							S	S	
					TH		TH	TH	
					TH		TH	TH	
					TH		TH		

BOTANICAL NAME	COMMON NAME
ZAMIACEAE	
Macrozamia douglasii W.Hill ex F.M.Bailey	zamia palm
Macrozamia pauli-guilielmi W.Hill & F.Muell.	
ZINGIBERACEAE	
Alpinia arundelliana (F.M.Bailey) K.Schum.	native ginger
Alpinia caerulea (R.Br.) Benth.	wild ginger

| | STRAND | | | LITTORAL FLAT | FORE DUNE | HIND DUNE | HIGH DUNE | | |
STATUS	GRASS LAND	SEDGE LAND	HERB LAND	LOW WOOD LAND	LOW OPEN FOREST	HEATH	WOOD LAND	OPEN FOREST	CLOSED FOREST
							P	P	
E							P	P	
					P				H
					P				H

INDEX TO SPECIES LIST

This is an index of Species and Common Names of plants listed by Family in alphabetical order in the Species List

SPECIES AND COMMON NAME	FAMILY	SPECIES AND COMMON NAME	FAMILY
Abrodictyum brassii	HYMENOPHYLLACEAE	*Acronychia laevis*	RUTACEAE
Abrodictyum caudatum	HYMENOPHYLLACEAE	*Acronychia pubescens*	RUTACEAE
Abrodictyum elongatum	HYMENOPHYLLACEAE	*Acronychia wilcoxiana*	RUTACEAE
Abrodictyum obscurum	HYMENOPHYLLACEAE	*Acrotriche aggregata*	ERICACEAE
Abrophyllum ornans var. *ornans*	CARPODETACEAE	*Actites megalocarpus*	ASTERACEAE
Abrus precatorius subsp. *africanus*	FABACEAE	*Adiantum hispidulum*	PTERIDACEAE
Acacia baueri subsp. *baueri*	MIMOSACEAE	*Adiantum hispidulum* var.	PTERIDACEAE
Acacia complanata	MIMOSACEAE	*hypoglaucum*	
Acacia concurrens	MIMOSACEAE	*Aegialitis annulata*	PLUMBAGINACEAE
Acacia disparrima	MIMOSACEAE	*Aegiceras corniculatum*	MYRSINACEAE
Acacia disparrima subsp.	MIMOSACEAE	African love grass	POACEAE
disparrima		*Agathis robusta*	ARAUCARIACEAE
Acacia falcata	MIMOSACEAE	*Ageratum conyzoides* subsp.	ASTERACEAE
Acacia falciformis	MIMOSACEAE	*conyzoides*	
Acacia fimbriata	MIMOSACEAE	*Agiortia pedicellata*	ERICACEAE
Acacia flavescens	MIMOSACEAE	*Ailanthus triphysa*	SIMAROUBACEAE
Acacia leiocalyx subsp.	MIMOSACEAE	*Aira cupaniana*	POACEAE
herveyensis		*Alectryon reticulatus*	SAPINDACEAE
Acacia leiocalyx subsp. *leiocalyx*	MIMOSACEAE	*Allocasuarina littoralis*	CASUARINACEAE
Acacia penninervis var.	MIMOSACEAE	*Allocasuarina torulosa*	CASUARINACEAE
longiracemosa		*Alloteropsis semialata*	POACEAE
Acacia quadrilateralis	MIMOSACEAE	*Alphitonia excelsa*	RHAMNACEAE
Acacia sophorae	MIMOSACEAE	*Alphitonia petriei*	RHAMNACEAE
Acacia suaveolens	MIMOSACEAE	*Alpinia arundelliana*	ZINGIBERACEAE
Acacia ulicifolia	MIMOSACEAE	*Alpinia caerulea*	ZINGIBERACEAE
Acanthospermum hispidum	ASTERACEAE	*Alyxia ruscifolia*	APOCYNACEAE
Acetosella vulgaris	POLYGONACEAE	*Amyema bifurcata*	LORANTHACEAE
Achyranthes aspera	AMARANTHACEAE	*Amyema cambagei*	LORANTHACEAE
Acianthus exsertus	ORCHIDACEAE	*Amyema congener*	LORANTHACEAE
Acianthus fornicatus	ORCHIDACEAE	*Amyema mackayensis*	LORANTHACEAE
Acianthus pusillus	ORCHIDACEAE	*Amyema miquelii*	LORANTHACEAE
Acmena hemilampra subsp.	MYRTACEAE	*Amylotheca dictyophleba*	LORANTHACEAE
hemilampra		*Andropogon virginicus*	POACEAE
Acmena smithii	MYRTACEAE	*Angiopteris evecta*	MARATTIACEAE
Acronychia imperforata	RUTACEAE	angled lobelia	CAMPANULACEAE

Angophora leiocarpa	MYRTACEAE	baconwood	MIMOSACEAE
Aotus ericoides	FABACEAE	*Bacopa monnieri*	PLANTAGINACEAE
Aotus lanigera	FABACEAE	*Baeckea frutescens*	MYRTACEAE
Apium prostratum	APIACEAE	*Baeckea linifolia*	MYRTACEAE
appressed bossiaea	FABACEAE	balloon cotton bush	APOCYNACEAE
Araucaria bidwillii	ARAUCARIACEAE	*Baloskion pallens*	RESTIONACEAE
Araucaria cunninghamii var.	ARAUCARIACEAE	*Baloskion tenuiculme*	RESTIONACEAE
cunninghamii		*Baloskion tetraphyllum* subsp.	RESTIONACEAE
Archidendron lovelliae	MIMOSACEAE	*meiostachyum*	
Archontophoenix cunninghamiana	ARECACEAE	*Banksia aemula*	PROTEACEAE
Argemone ochroleuca subsp.	PAPAVERACEAE	*Banksia integrifolia* subsp. *compar*	PROTACEAE
ochroleuca		*Banksia integrifolia* subsp.	PROTEACEAE
Argentine peppercress	BRASSICACEAE	*integrifolia*	
Aristida benthamii var. *benthamii*	POACEAE	*Banksia oblongifolia*	PROTEACEAE
Aristida calycina var. *calycina*	POACEAE	*Banksia robur*	PROTEACEAE
Aristida holathera var. *hlathera*	POACEAE	*Banksia serrata*	PROTEACEAE
arrowroot orchid	ORCHIDACEAE	barb wire grass	POACEAE
Artanema fimbricatum	SCROPHULARIACEAE	barb wire vine	SMILACACEAE
Arthrochilus irritabilis	ORCHIDACEAE	bare twigrush	CYPERACEAE
Arthropteris tenella	TECTARIACEAE	barnyard grass	POACEAE
Asclepias curassavica	APOCYNACEAE	basket fern	POLYPODIACEAE
ash quandong	ELAEOCARPACEAE	bastard summer grass	POACEAE
Asian bladderwort	LENTIBULARIACEAE	bats-wing fern	DENNSTAEDTIACEAE
Asian mustard	BRASSICACEAE	*Bauera capitata*	CUNONIACEAE
Asplenium australasicum	ASPLENIACEAE	*Baumea arthrophylla*	CYPERACEAE
Asplenium polyodon	ASPLENIACEAE	*Baumea articulata*	CYPERACEAE
Astrotricha glabra	ARALIACEAE	*Baumea juncea*	CYPERACEAE
Astrotricha longifolia	ARALIACEAE	*Baumea muelleri*	CYPERACEAE
Atractocarpus chartaceus	RUBIACEAE	*Baumea rubiginosa*	CYPERACEAE
Australian blue bell	CAMPANULACEAE	*Baumea teretifolia*	CYPERACEAE
Austromyrtus dulcis	MYRTACEAE	beach acronychia	RUTACEAE
Austrosteenisia blackii var. *blackii*	FABACEAE	beach calophyllum	CLUSIACEAE
autumn green orchid	ORCHIDACEAE	beach lepturus	POACEAE
Avicennia marina subsp.	ACANTHACEAE	beach primrose	ONAGRACEAE
australasica		beach sow thistle	ASTERACEAE
avocado	LAURACEAE	beach spinefix	POACEAE
Axonopus compressus	POACEAE	beach vigna	FABACEAE
Axonopus fissifolius	POACEAE	beach wattle	MIMOSACEAE
baby blue eyes	CONVOLVULACEAE	beetle orchid	ORCHIDACEAE
Backhousia citriodora	MYRTACEAE	*Beilschmiedia elliptica*	LAURACEAE
Backhousia myrtifolia	MYRTACEAE	*Beilschmiedia obtusifolia*	LAURACEAE

bennet's ash	RUTACEAE	boronia	RUTACEAE
Bidens pilosa	ASTERACEAE	*Boronia bipinnata*	RUTACEAE
Bidens pilosa var. *pilosa*	ASTERACEAE	*Boronia falcifolia*	RUTACEAE
bindy	ASTERACEAE	*Boronia occidentalis*	RUTACEAE
bitou bush	ASTERACEAE	*Boronia parviflora*	RUTACEAE
bitter broom	SCROPHULARIACEAE	*Boronia rivularis*	RUTACEAE
bitter pea	FABACEAE	*Boronia rosmarinifolia*	RUTACEAE
bitter pea	FABACEAE	*Bossiaea brownii*	FABACEAE
black apple	SAPOTACEAE	*Bossiaea concolor*	FABACEAE
black ebony	EBENACEAE	*Bossiaea ensata*	FABACEAE
black mangrove	COMBRETACEAE	*Bossiaea heterophylla*	FABACEAE
black she oak	CASUARINACEAE	*Bossiaea rupicola*	FABACEAE
black wattle	MIMOSACEAE	box mistletoe	LORANTHACEAE
blackberry nightshade	SOLANACEAE	*Brachychiton populneus* subsp. *populneus*	STERCULIACEAE
blackbutt	MYRTACEAE		
black-eyed susan	ELAEOCARPACEAE	*Brachyloma daphnoides* subsp. *daphnoides*	ERICACEAE
blackrod	OROBANCHACEAE		
blackseed samphire	CHENOPODIACEAE	*Brachyloma scortechinii*	ERICACEAE
blady grass	POACEAE	*Brassica tournefortii*	BRASSICACEAE
Blandfordia grandiflora	BLANDFORDIACEAE	Brazilian fireweed	ASTERACEAE
Blechnum camfieldii	BLECHNACEAE	*Breynia oblongifolia*	PHYLLANTHACEAE
Blechnum cartilagineum	BLECHNACEAE	bristly tree fern	DICKSONIACEAE
Blechnum indicum	BLECHNACEAE	brittlewood	EUPHORBIACEAE
blind your-eye mangrove	EUPHORBIACEAE	*Briza maxima*	POACEAE
blood vine	FABACEAE	*Briza minor*	POACEAE
bloodroot	HEMODORACEAE	broad wedge pea	FABACEAE
blue bladderwort	LENTIBULARIACEAE	broad-leaf carpet grass	POACEAE
blue dampiera	GOODENIACEAE	broadleaf paspalum	POACEAE
blue flax lily	HEMEROCALLIDACEAE	broad-leafed lilly	LAXMANNIACEAE
blue lilly pilly	MYRTACEAE	broad-leaved banksia	PROTEACEAE
blue pimpernel	MYRSINACEAE	broad-leaved boxwood	CELASTRACEAE
blue quandong	ELAEOCARPACEAE	broad-leaved hickory	MIMOSACEAE
blue tongue	MELASTOMATACEAE	broad-leaved lilly pilly	MYRTACEAE
blueberry ash	ELAEOCARPACEAE	*Bromus catharticus*	POACEAE
blueberry lilly	HEMEROCALLIDACEAE	brown birch	FLACOURTIACEAE
blue-eyed grass	IRIDACEAE	brown bolly gum	LAURACEAE
bogrush	CYPERACEAE	brown myrtle	MYRTACEAE
bolly gum	LAURACEAE	brown pine	PODOCARPACEAE
bolwarra	EUPOMATIACEAE	brown walnut	LAURACEAE
bonnet orchid	ORCHIDACEAE	brown's love grass	POACEAE
bordered panic	POACEAE	*Bruguiera gymnorhiza*	RHIZOPHORACEAE

149

brush box	MYRTACEAE
brush pepperbush	WINTERACEAE
Buchnera urticifolia	OROBANCHACEAE
Bulbophyllum schillerianum	ORCHIDACEAE
Bulbostylis barbata	CYPERACEAE
bumpy ash	RUTACEAE
bunchy sedge	CYPERACEAE
bundled guinea flower	DILLENIACEAE
bunya pine	ARAUCARIACEAE
Burchardia umbellata	COLCHICACEAE
Burdekin plum	ANACARDIACEAE
Burmannia disticha	BURMANNIACEAE
burney vine	MORACEAE
bush coondoo	SAPOTACEAE
bush iris	IRIDACEAE
bush lemon	RUTACEAE
bush pea	FABACEAE
button wood	PHYLLANTHACEAE
cabbage tree palm	ARECACEAE
Caesalpinia bonduc	CAESALPINIACEAE
Caesalpinia scortechinii	CAESALPINIACEAE
Cakile edentula	BRASSICACEAE
Caladenia alata	ORCHIDACEAE
Caladenia carnea	ORCHIDACEAE
Caladenia catenata	ORCHIDACEAE
Caladenia fuscata	ORCHIDACEAE
Calanthe triplicata	ORCHIDACEAE
Caleana major	ORCHIDACEAE
Callerya megasperma	FABACEAE
Callitris columellaris	CUPRESSACEAE
Callitris macleayana	CUPRESSACEAE
Callitris rhomboidea	CUPRESSACEAE
Calochilus grandiflorus	ORCHIDACEAE
Calochlaena dubia	DICKSONIACEAE
Calophyllum inophyllum	CLUSIACEAE
Calystegia soldanella	CONVOLVULACEAE
Canadian fleabane	ASTERACEAE
Canarium australasicum	BURSERACEAE
canary beech	ANNONACEAE
Canavalia rosea	FABACEAE
candlewood	LAURACEAE

cannonball mangrove	MELIACEAE
Carex pumila	CYPERACEAE
Carpobrotus aequilaterus	AIZOACEAE
Carpobrotus glaucescens	AIZOACEAE
carrol	MYRTACEAE
Cassytha filiformis	LAURACEAE
Cassytha glabella	LAURACEAE
Cassytha muelleri	LAURACEAE
Cassytha paniculata	LAURACEAE
Cassytha pubescens	LAURACEAE
Casuarina equisetifolia subsp. *incana*	CASUARINACEAE
Casuarina glauca	CASUARINACEAE
Caustis blakei subsp. *blakei*	CYPERACEAE
Caustis recurvata	CYPERACEAE
celerywood	ARALIACEAE
Celtis paniculata	ULMACEAE
Cenchrus echinatus	POACEAE
Centella asiatica	APIACEAE
centrolepis	CENTROLEPIDACEAE
Centrolepis exserta	CENTROLEPIDACEAE
Centrolepis strigosa	CENTROLEPIDACEAE
Cephalaralia cephalobotrys	ARALIACEAE
Cerastium glomeratum	CAROPHYLLACEAE
Ceriops australis	RHIZOPHORACEAE
chaff flower	AMARANTHACEAE
chain fruit	APOCYNACEAE
Chamaecrista nomame	CAESALPINIACEAE
cheese tree	PHYLLANTHACEAE
chick weed	ASTERACEAE
chickweed	CAROPHYLLACEAE
Chiloglottis diphylla	ORCHIDACEAE
Chiloglottis sylvestris	ORCHIDACEAE
chinnock	SCROPHULARIACEAE
Chloanthes parviflora	LAMIACEAE
Chloris gayana	POACEAE
Chloris inflata	POACEAE
Choretrum candollei	SANTALACEAE
Christella dentata	THELYPTERIDACEAE
Christmas bells	BLANDFORDIACEAE
Christmas orchid	ORCHIDACEAE

Chrysanthemoides monilifera subsp. *rotundata*	ASTERACEAE	*Coelospermum paniculatum* var. *paniculatum*	RUBIACEAE
Chrysocephalum apiculatum	ASTERACEAE	coffee bush	PHYLLANTHACEAE
Cinnamomum baileyanum	LAURACEAE	*Coleocarya gracilis*	RESTIONACEAE
Cinnamomum oliveri	LAURACEAE	Columbian waxweed	LYTHRACEAE
Cirsium vulgare	ASTERACEAE	comb fern	SCHIZAEACEAE
Cissus hypoglauca	VITACEAE	*Comesperma defoliatum*	POLYGALACEAE
Cissus sterculiifolia	VITACEAE	*Comesperma retusum*	POLYGALACEAE
Citrus x limon	RUTACEAE	*Commelina diffusa*	COMMELINACEAE
Cladium procerum	CYPERACEAE	common aotus	FABACEAE
Claoxylon australe	EUPHORBIACEAE	common bracken fern	DENNSTAEDTIACEAE
Clematicissus opaca	VITACEAE	common catchfly	CAROPHYLLACEAE
Clematis glycinoides	RANUNCULACEAE	common finger rush	CYPERACEAE
Clematis pickeringii	RANUNCULACEAE	common heath	ERICACEAE
Clerodendrum floribundum	LAMIACEAE	common lomandra	LAXMANNIACEAE
climbing fishbone fern	TECTARIACEAE	common passionfruit	PASSIFLORACEAE
climbing orchid	ORCHIDACEAE	common prickly pear	CACTACEAE
climbing panax	ARALIACEAE	common reed	POACEAE
climbing pandanus	PANDANACEAE	common sowthistle	ASTERACEAE
Clivia sp.	AMARYLLIDACEAE	common thistle	ASTERACEAE
club bogmoss	LYCOPODIACEAE	common wasp orchid	ORCHIDACEAE
club mangrove	PLUMBAGINACEAE	conesticks	PROTEACEAE
clubrush	CYPERACEAE	*Conospermum taxifolium*	PROTEACEAE
clustered bauera	CUNONIACEAE	*Conyza canadensis*	ASTERACEAE
clustered copper-wire daisy	ASTERACEAE	*Conyza parva*	ASTERACEAE
clustered love grass	POACEAE	*Conyza sumatrensis*	ASTERACEAE
coast bearded heath	ERICACEAE	Cooloola ironwood	MYRTACEAE
coast stackhousia	STACKHOUSIACEAE	copper beard orchid	ORCHIDACEAE
coastal banksia	PROTEACEAE	coral fern	LYCOPODIACEAE
coastal boobiala	SCROPHULARIACEAE	coral heath	ERICACEAE
coastal dune digitaria	POACEAE	cord-rush	RESTIONACEAE
coastal dune love grass	POACEAE	corduroy tamarind	SAPINDACEAE
coastal jack bean	FABACEAE	cordyline	LAXMANNIACEAE
coastal pseudanthus	PICRODENRACEAE	*Cordyline rubra*	LAXMANNIACEAE
coastal she oak	CASUARINACEAE	*Cordyline terminalis*	LAXMANNIACEAE
coastal sprite orchid,	ORCHIDACEAE	corky passion flower	PASSIFLORACEAE
cobbler's pegs	ASTERACEAE	*Coronidium elatum* subsp. *elatum*	ASTERACEAE
cockatoo grass	POACEAE	*Coronidium oxylepis* subsp. *carnosum*	ASTERACEAE
cockspur flower	LAMIACEAE	*Corunastylis acuminata*	ORCHIDACEAE
cocky apple	LECYTHIDACEAE	*Corybas undulatus*	ORCHIDACEAE

Corymbia gummifera	MYRTACEAE	*Cyperus eglobosus*	CYPERACEAE
Corymbia intermedia	MYRTACEAE	*Cyperus enervis*	CYPERACEAE
Corymbia tessellaris	MYRTACEAE	*Cyperus haspan*	CYPERACEAE
cotton tree	MALVACEAE	*Cyperus laevigatus*	CYPERACEAE
crabapple	CUNONIACEAE	*Cyperus lucidus*	CYPERACEAE
crabs eye creeper	FABACEAE	*Cyperus pedunculosus*	CYPERACEAE
Crassocephalum crepidioides	ASTERACEAE	*Cyperus polystachyos* var.	CYPERACEAE
creeping phyllanthus	PHYLLANTHACEAE	*polystachyos*	
creeping oxalis	OXALIDACEAE	*Cyperus scaber*	CYPERACEAE
creeping shade grass	POACEAE	*Cyperus stoloniferus*	CYPERACEAE
Crepidomanes saxifragoides	HYMENOPHYLLACEAE	*Cyperus stradbrokensis*	CYPERACEAE
Crinum pedunculatum	AMARYLLIDACEAE	cypress mistletoe	LORANTHACEAE
Crotalaria brevis	FABACEAE	dalrymple vigna	FABACEAE
Crotalaria pallida var. *obovata*	FABACEAE	*Dampiera stricta*	GOODENIACEAE
crows nest fern	ASPLENIACEAE	*Dampiera sylvestris*	GOODENIACEAE
crowsfoot grass	POACEAE	daphne heath	ERICACEAE
Cryptocarya foetida	LAURACEAE	dark greenhood orchid	ORCHIDACEAE
Cryptocarya glaucescens	LAURACEAE	dark wire grass	POACEAE
Cryptocarya macdonaldii	LAURACEAE	*Daviesia acicularis*	FABACEAE
Cryptostylis erecta	ORCHIDACEAE	*Daviesia umbellulata*	FABACEAE
cudweed	ASTERACEAE	*Decaspermum humile*	MYRTACEAE
Cupaniopsis anacardioides	SAPINDACEAE	*Dendrobium aemulum*	ORCHIDACEAE
Cuphea carthagenensis	LYTHRACEAE	*Dendrobium gracilicaule*	ORCHIDACEAE
curly wigs	CYPERACEAE	*Dendrobium speciosum*	ORCHIDACEAE
curracabah	MIMOSACEAE	*Dendrobium tetragonum*	ORCHIDACEAE
Cyanthillium cinereum	ASTERACEAE	*Dendrophthoe glabrescens*	LORANTHACEAE
Cyathea cooperi	CYATHEACEAE	*Denhamia celastroides*	CELASTRACEAE
Cyathea leichhardtiana	CYATHEACEAE	*Desmodium nemorosum*	FABACEAE
Cyclophyllum coprosmoides var.	RUBIACEAE	devils rice	PROTEACEAE
spathulatum		*Dianella caerulea* var. *protensa*	HEMEROCALLIDACEAE
Cyclophyllum longipetalum	RUBIACEAE	*Dianella caerulea* var. *vannata*	HEMEROCALLIDACEAE
Cyclospermum leptophyllum	APIACEAE	*Dianella congesta*	HEMEROCALLIDACEAE
Cycnogeton procerus	JUNCAGINACEAE	*Dianella crinoides*	HEMEROCALLIDACEAE
Cymbidium madidum	ORCHIDACEAE	*Dianella longifolia*	HEMEROCALLIDACEAE
Cymbidium suave	ORCHIDACEAE	*Dicksonia youngiae*	DICKSONIACEAE
Cymbopogon refractus	POACEAE	*Dicranopteris linearis* var. *linearis*	GLEICHENIACEAE
Cynanchum carnosum	APOCYNACEAE	*Digitaria ciliaris*	POACEAE
Cynodon dactylon var. *dactylon*	POACEAE	*Digitaria didactyla*	POACEAE
Cyperus brevifolius	CYPERACEAE	*Digitaria leucostachya*	POACEAE
Cyperus conicus	CYPERACEAE	*Digitaria parviflora*	POACEAE
Cyperus cyperoides	CYPERACEAE	*Digitaria violascens*	POACEAE

Dillwynia floribunda	FABACEAE	*Dysphania ambrosioides*	CHENOPODIACEAE
Dillwynia retorta	FABACEAE	early spring grass	POACEAE
Dioscorea transversa	DIOSCOREACEAE	*Echinochloa crus-galli*	POACEAE
Diospyros pentamera	EBENACEAE	*Echinochloa telmatophila*	POACEAE
Diplachne fusca var. *fusca*	POACEAE	*Eclipta prostrata*	ASTERACEAE
Dipodium variegatum	ORCHIDACEAE	*Elaeocarpus eumundi*	ELAEOCARPACEAE
Diteilis simmondsii	ORCHIDACEAE	*Elaeocarpus grandis*	ELAEOCARPACEAE
Diuris alba	ORCHIDACEAE	*Elaeocarpus obovatus*	ELAEOCARPACEAE
Diuris aurea	ORCHIDACEAE	*Elaeocarpus reticulatus*	ELAEOCARPACEAE
Dockrillia bowmanii	ORCHIDACEAE	elastic grass	POACEAE
Dockrillia linguiformis	ORCHIDACEAE	*Elattostachys nervosa*	SAPINDACEAE
Dockrillia mortii	ORCHIDACEAE	*Eleocharis cylindrostachys*	CYPERACEAE
dodder	LAURACEAE	*Eleocharis difformis*	CYPERACEAE
dodder laurel	LAURACEAE	*Eleocharis equisetina*	CYPERACEAE
Dodonaea triquetra	SAPINDACEAE	*Eleocharis geniculata*	CYPERACEAE
Dodonaea viscosa subsp. *burmanniana*	SAPINDACEAE	*Eleocharis ochrostachys*	CYPERACEAE
		Eleocharis sphacelata	CYPERACEAE
Dodonaea viscosa subsp. *viscosa*	SAPINDACEAE	*Eleusine indica*	POACEAE
dogwood	FABACEAE	*Elionurus citreus*	POACEAE
domatia tree	LAURACEAE	elkhorn	POLYPODIACEAE
don't panic	POACEAE	embelia	MYRSINACEAE
dotted sun orchid	ORCHIDACEAE	*Embelia australiana*	MYRSINACEAE
downy bossiaea	FABACEAE	*Emilia sonchifolia* var. *javanica*	ASTERACEAE
downy devil's vine	LAURACEAE	*Emilia sonchifolia* var. *sonchifolia*	ASTERACEAE
Drosera binata	DROSERACEAE	*Emmenosperma alphitonioides*	RHAMNACEAE
Drosera finlaysoniana	DROSERACEAE	*Emmenosperma cunninghamii*	RHAMNACEAE
Drosera lunata	DROSERACEAE	*Empodisma minus*	RESTIONACEAE
Drosera pygmaea	DROSERACEAE	*Endiandra discolor*	LAURACEAE
Drosera spatulata	DROSERACEAE	*Endiandra sieberi*	LAURACEAE
Drosera spatulata var. *spatulata*	DROSERACEAE	*Entolasia marginata*	POACEAE
Drynaria rigidula	POLYPODIACEAE	*Entolasia stricta*	POACEAE
Duboisia myoporoides	SOLANACEAE	*Entolasia whiteana*	POACEAE
dune cypress pine	CUPRESSACEAE	*Enydra woolsii*	ASTERACEAE
dune fan flower	GOODENIACEAE	*Epacris microphylla* var. *microphylla*	ERICACEAE
dusky coral pea	FABACEAE		
dusky fingers	ORCHIDACEAE	*Epacris obtusifolia*	ERICACEAE
dutch millet	POACEAE	*Epacris pulchella*	ERICACEAE
dwarf banksia	PROTEACEAE	*Eragrostis brownii*	POACEAE
dwarf cassia	CAESALPINIACEAE	*Eragrostis curvula*	POACEAE
dwarf's umbrella	RUBIACEAE	*Eragrostis elongata*	POACEAE
Dysoxylum rufum	MELIACEAE	*Eragrostis interrupta*	POACEAE

Eragrostis parviflora	POACEAE		*Eupomatia bennettii*	EUPOMATIACEAE
Eragrostis spartinoides	POACEAE		*Eupomatia laurina*	EUPOMATIACEAE
Eragrostis tenuifolia	POACEAE		*Euroshinus falcata*	ANACARDIACEAE
Erechtites valerianifolius forma *valerianifolius*	ASTERACEAE		*Eustrephus latifolius*	LAXMANNIACEAE
			everlasting daisy	ASTERACEAE
erect guinea flower	DILLENIACEAE		*Evolvulus alsinoides*	CONVOLVULACEAE
erect maroonhood	ORCHIDACEAE		*Excoecaria agallocha*	EUPHORBIACEAE
erect mistletoe	LORANTHACEAE		*Exocarpos cupressiformis*	SANTALACEAE
Eremochloa bimaculata	POACEAE		fairy orchid	ORCHIDACEAE
Eriachne glabrata	POACEAE		false bracken fern	DICKSONIACEAE
Eriachne insularis	POACEAE		false parrot pea	FABACEAE
Eriachne pallescens	POACEAE		fan flower	GOODENIACEAE
Eriachne pallescens var. *gracilis*	POACEAE		feather plant	RESTIONACEAE
Eriachne pallescens var. *pallescens*	POACEAE		feathered bearded heath	ERICACEAE
			Ficinia nodosa	CYPERACEAE
Eriachne rara	POACEAE		*Ficus fraseri*	MORACEAE
Erigeron pusillus	ASTERACEAE		*Ficus obliqua*	MORACEAE
Erigeron sumatrensis	ASTERACEAE		*Ficus opposita*	MORACEAE
Eriocaulon australe	ERIOCAULACEAE		*Ficus rubiginosa* forma *glabrescens*	MORACEAE
Eriocaulon scariosum	ERIOCAULACEAE			
Eriochloa fatmensis	POACEAE		*Ficus watkinsiana*	MORACEAE
Eriochloa procera	POACEAE		*Fimbristylis dichotoma*	CYPERACEAE
Eriostemon australasius	RUTACEAE		*Fimbristylis ferruginea*	CYPERACEAE
Erythrorchis cassythoides	ORCHIDACEAE		*Fimbristylis nutans*	CYPERACEAE
Eucalyptus grandis	MYRTACEAE		*Fimbristylis polytrichoides*	CYPERACEAE
Eucalyptus hallii	MYRTACEAE		fine-leafed mat rush	LAXMANNIACEAE
Eucalyptus latisinensis	MYRTACEAE		fire grass	POACEAE
Eucalyptus microcorys	MYRTACEAE		fishbone fern	LOMARIOPSIDACEAE
Eucalyptus pilularis	MYRTACEAE		five-leaved water vine	VITACEAE
Eucalyptus planchoniana	MYRTACEAE		*Flagellaria indica*	FLAGELLARIACEAE
Eucalyptus racemosa subsp. *racemosa*	MYRTACEAE		flannelweed	MALVACEAE
			flat mistletoe	VISCACEAE
Eucalyptus resinifera	MYRTACEAE		flat-stemmed wattle	MIMOSACEAE
Eucalyptus robusta	MYRTACEAE		flax lilly	HEMEROCALLIDACEAE
Eucalyptus robusta x *E. tereticornis*	MYRTACEAE		*Flindersia bennettii*	RUTACEAE
			Flindersia schottiana	RUTACEAE
Eucalyptus siderophloia	MYRTACEAE		floating bladderwort	LENTIBULARIACEAE
Eucalyptus tereticornis	MYRTACEAE		flooded gum	MYRTACEAE
Eumundi quandong	ELAEOCARPACEAE		fluke bogrush	CYPERACEAE
Euphorbia cyathophora	EUPHORBIACEAE		flying duck orchid	ORCHIDACEAE
Euphorbia hyssopifolia	EUPHORBIACEAE		foam bark tree	SAPINDACEAE

154

forest boronia	RUTACEAE
forest clematis	RANUNCULACEAE
forest grass tree	XANTHORRHOEACEAE
forest lobelia	CAMPANULACEAE
forest oak	CASUARINACEAE
forest olive	OLEACEAE
forest red gum	MYRTACEAE
fork sundew	DROSERACEAE
forked burmannia	BURMANNIACEAE
four-leaf allseed	CAROPHYLLACEAE
foxtail	CYPERACEAE
fragrant climbing fern	POLYPODIACEAE
Fraser Island broom heath	ERICACEAE
Fraser Island creeper	BIGNONIACEAE
Fraser Island satinay	MYRTACEAE
Freycinetia scandens	PANDANACEAE
fringed lilly	LAXMANNIACEAE
fringed wattle	MIMOSACEAE
frog fruit	VERBENACEAE
Gahnia clarkei	CYPERACEAE
Gahnia sieberiana	CYPERACEAE
Galinsoga parviflora	ASTERACEAE
Gamochaeta pensylvanica	ASTERACEAE
geebung	PROTEACEAE
Geitonoplesium cymosum	HEMEROCALLIDACEAE
Genoplesium psammophilum	ORCHIDACEAE
Genoplesium pumilum	ORCHIDACEAE
Genoplesium sp.	ORCHIDACEAE
Geodorum densiflorum	ORCHIDACEAE
giant fern	MARATTIACEAE
giant Paramatta grass	POACEAE
giant pepper vine	PIPERACEAE
Gleichenia dicarpa	GLEICHENIACEAE
Gleichenia mendellii	GLEICHENIACEAE
Glochidion ferdinandi	PHYLLANTHACEAE
Glochidion lobocarpum	PHYLLANTHACEAE
Glochidion sumatranum	PHYLLANTHACEAE
Gloriosa superba	COLCHICACEAE
glory lilly	COLCHICACEAE
Glossocardia bidens	ASTERACEAE
Glossodia minor	ORCHIDACEAE

glossy acronychia	RUTACEAE
glossy nightshade	SOLANACEAE
Glycine clandestina var. *clandestina*	FABACEAE
glycine pea	FABACEAE
Glycine tabacina	FABACEAE
Glycine tomentella	FABACEAE
Gmelina leichhardtii	LAMIACEAE
goat's foot	CONVOLVULACEAE
golden diuris	ORCHIDACEAE
golden everlasting daisy	ASTERACEAE
golden fern	PTERIDACEAE
golden mistletoe	LORANTHACEAE
golden mistletoe	VISCACEAE
Gomphocarpus physocarpus	APOCYNACEAE
Gompholobium latifolium	FABACEAE
Gompholobium pinnatum	FABACEAE
Gompholobium virgatum	FABACEAE
Gomphrena celosioides	AMARANTHACEAE
Gonocarpus micranthus subsp. *ramosissimus*	HALORAGACEAE
goodenia	GOODENIACEAE
Goodenia rotundifolia	GOODENIACEAE
Goodenia stelligera	GOODENIACEAE
grass tree	XANTHORRHOEACEAE
grass-trigger plant	STYLIDACEAE
great quaking grass	POACEAE
green couch	POACEAE
green five corners	ERICACEAE
green midge orchid	ORCHIDACEAE
green tamarind	SAPINDACEAE
greenhood orchid	ORCHIDACEAE
green-leaved silkpod	APOCYNACEAE
Grevillea reptans	PROTEACEAE
Grevillea robusta	PROTEACEAE
grey ash	RHAMNACEAE
grey ironbark	MYRTACEAE
grey mangrove	ACANTHACEAE
grey rush	CYPERACEAE
gristle fern	BLECHNACEAE
Guilleminea densa	AMARANTHACEAE

guinea flower	DILLENIACEAE
Guioa acutifolia	SAPINDACEAE
Gymnostachys anceps	ARECEAE
Gynochthodes canthoides	RUBIACEAE
Gynochthodes jasminoides	RUBIACEAE
Gynochthodes umbellata	RUBIACEAE
Haemodorum tenuifolium	HEMODORACEAE
hair grass	POACEAE
hairy acronychia	RUTACEAE
hairy bush pea	FABACEAE
hairy guinea flower	DILLENIACEAE
hairy jewel orchid	ORCHIDACEAE
hairy panic	POACEAE
hairy parrot pea	FABACEAE
hairy pigweed	PORTULACEAE
hairy pittosporum	PITTOSPORACEAE
hairy psychotria	RUBIACEAE
hairy rosewood	MELIACEAE
Hakea actites	PROTEACEAE
Halfordia kendack	RUTACEAE
Halodule uninervis	CYMODOEACEAE
handsome flat pea	FABACEAE
Haplopteris ensiformis	PTERIDACEAE
hard bolly gum	LAURACEAE
hard corkwood	LAURACEAE
Hardenbergia violacea	FABACEAE
Harnieria hygrophiloides	ACANTHACEAE
Harpullia alata	SAPINDACEAE
Harpullia pendula	SAPINDACEAE
hatpins	XYRIDACEAE
heart-leaf vine	MENISPERMACEAE
heath platysace	APIACEAE
heathy mirbelia	FABACEAE
hen and chicken	PHYLLANTHACEAE
herb of grace	PLANTAGINACEAE
Hibbertia acicularis	DILLENIACEAE
Hibbertia fasciculata	DILLENIACEAE
Hibbertia linearis	DILLENIACEAE
Hibbertia linearis var. *floribunda*	DILLENIACEAE
Hibbertia salicifolia	DILLENIACEAE
Hibbertia scandens	DILLENIACEAE

Hibbertia stricta	DILLENIACEAE
Hibbertia vestita var. *vestita*	DILLENIACEAE
Hibiscus diversifolius subsp. *diversifolius*	MALVACEAE
Hibiscus tiliaceus	MALVACEAE
hickory wattle	MIMOSACEAE
Hippocratea barbata	CELASTRACEAE
Histiopteris incisa	DENNSTAEDTIACEAE
Homalanthus populifolius	EUPHORBIACEAE
Homoranthus virgatus	MYRTACEAE
hoop pine	ARAUCARIACEAE
horseweed	ASTERACEAE
Hovea acutifolia	FABACEAE
Hovea clavata	FABACEAE
Hovea similis	FABACEAE
hoya	APOCYNACEAE
Hoya australis subsp. *australis*	APOCYNACEAE
hyacinth orchid	ORCHIDACEAE
Hybanthus monopetalus	VIOLACEAE
Hybanthus stellariodes	VIOLACEAE
Hydrocotyle acutiloba	ARALIACEAE
Hydrocotyle bonariensis	ARALIACEAE
Hydrocotyle verticillata	ARALIACEAE
Hypericum gramineum	CLUSIACEAE
Hypolaena fastigiata	RESTIONACEAE
Hypserpa decumbens	MENISPERMACEAE
Imperata cylindrica	POACEAE
Indian weed	ASTERACEAE
Indogofera hirsuta	FABACEAE
Ipomoea cairica	CONVOLVULACEAE
Ipomoea littoralis	CONVOLVULACEAE
Ipomoea pes-caprae subsp. *brasiliensis*	CONVOLVULACEAE
ironbark orchid	ORCHIDACEAE
Ischaemum australe var. *australe*	POACEAE
Ischaemum fragile	POACEAE
Ischaemum muticum	POACEAE
Ischaemum triticeum	POACEAE
ivory basswood	ARALIACEAE
Jacksonia scoparia	FABACEAE
Jacksonia stackhousei	FABACEAE

156

jackwood	LAURACEAE
Jagera pseudorhus var. *pseudorhus*	SAPINDACEAE
jellybean plant	CHENOPODIACEAE
jersey cudweed	ASTERACEAE
johnson's satinash	MYRTACEAE
jointed twigrush	CYPERACEAE
Juncus continuus	JUNCACEAE
Juncus kraussii	JUNCACEAE
jungle bristle fern	HYMENOPHYLLACEAE
kangaroo grass	POACEAE
Kennedia rubicunda	FABACEAE
kerosene bush	FABACEAE
king fern	OSMUNDACEAE
king greenhood	ORCHIDACEAE
king orchid	ORCHIDACEAE
knotty club rush	CYPERACEAE
knottybutt grass	POACEAE
knotvine	CELASTRACEAE
kurrajong	STERCULIACEAE
ladies slipper	VIOLACEAE
lanoline-bush	RUTACEAE
lantana	VERBENACEAE
Lantana camara	VERBENACEAE
large blue grass	POACEAE
large flower bush pea	FABACEAE
large mock-olive	OLEACEAE
large pricklevine	CAESALPINIACEAE
large-leaved hop bush	SAPINDACEAE
large-leaved wilkiea	MONIMIACEAE
Laxmannia compacta	LAXMANNIACEAE
Laxmannia gracilis	LAXMANNIACEAE
leafless bossiaea	FABACEAE
leafless milkwort	POLYGALACEAE
leafy elbow orchid	ORCHIDACEAE
leafy twigbush	CYPERACEAE
Leersia hexandra	POACEAE
lemon ironwood	MYRTACEAE
lemon scented tea tree	MYRTACEAE
lemon-scented grass	POACEAE
Lepidium bonariense	BRASSICACEAE

Lepidium virginicum	BRASSICACEAE
Lepidosperma laterale	CYPERACEAE
Lepidosperma longitudinale	CYPERACEAE
Lepironia articulata	CYPERACEAE
Leptocarpus tenax	RESTIONACEAE
Leptomeria acida	SANTALACEAE
Leptospermum juniperinum	MYRTACEAE
Leptospermum liversidgei	MYRTACEAE
Leptospermum petersonii	MYRTACEAE
Leptospermum polygalifolium	MYRTACEAE
Leptospermum semibaccatum	MYRTACEAE
Leptospermum speciosum	MYRTACEAE
Leptospermum trinervium	MYRTACEAE
Lepturus repens	POACEAE
Leucopogon leptospermoides	ERICACEAE
Leucopogon margarodes	ERICACEAE
Leucopogon parviflorus	ERICACEAE
Leucopogon pimeleoides	ERICACEAE
lillypilly satinash	MYRTACEAE
lily	AMARYLLIDACEAE
Limonium solanderi	PLUMBAGINACEAE
Lindsaea brachypoda	LINDSAEACEAE
Lindsaea ensifolia subsp. *agati*	LINDSAEACEAE
Lindsaea ensifolia subsp. *ensifolia*	LINDSAEACEAE
Lindsaea incisa	LINDSAEACEAE
Lindsaea repens	LINDSAEACEAE
Lindsaea repens var. *marquesensis*	LINDSAEACEAE
Linospadix monostachyos	ARECACEAE
Litsea australis	LAURACEAE
Litsea reticulata	LAURACEAE
little quaking grass	POACEAE
Livistona australis	ARECACEAE
Livistona decora	ARECACEAE
Lobelia anceps	CAMPANULACEAE
Lobelia purpurascens	CAMPANULACEAE
Lobelia trigonocaulis	CAMPANULACEAE
Lolium rigidum	POACEAE
Lomandra confertifolia subsp. *pallida*	LAXMANNIACEAE
Lomandra elongata	LAXMANNIACEAE

157

Lomandra filiformis subsp. filiformis	LAXMANNIACEAE	Melaleuca pachyphylla	MYRTACEAE
Lomandra laxa	LAXMANNIACEAE	Melaleuca quinquenervia	MYRTACEAE
Lomandra longifolia	LAXMANNIACEAE	Melastoma malabathricum subsp. malabathricum	MELASTOMATACEAE
Lomandra multiflora subsp. multiflora	LAXMANNIACEAE	Melia azedarach	MELIACEAE
long -leaf water vine	VITACEAE	Melicope elleryana	RUTACEAE
long-flowered evening primrose	ONAGRACEAE	Melicope vitiflora	RUTACEAE
long-flowered mistletoe	LORANTHACEAE	Melinis repens	POACEAE
long-leaved pandanus	PANDANACEAE	Melodinus australis	APOCYNACEAE
Lophostemon confertus	MYRTACEAE	Melodorum leichhardtii	ANNONACEAE
Lophostemon suaveolens	MYRTACEAE	Mexican poppy	PAPAVERACEAE
lotononis	FABACEAE	Microsorum maximum	POLYPODIACEAE
Lotononis bainesii	FABACEAE	Microsorum punctatum	POLYPODIACEAE
love grass	POACEAE	Microsorum scandens	POLYPODIACEAE
Lumnitzera racemosa	COMBRETACEAE	Microtis parviflora	ORCHIDACEAE
Lycopodiella cernua	LYCOPODIACEAE	midgen berry	MYRTACEAE
Lycopodiella lateralis	LYCOPODIACEAE	milk maids	COLCHICACEAE
Lycopodiella serpentina	LYCOPODIACEAE	milk vine	APOCYNACEAE
Lygodium microphyllum	SCHIZAEACEAE	minute orchid	ORCHIDACEAE
Lysimachia arvensis	MYRSINACEAE	Mirbelia rubiifolia	FABACEAE
Macarthuria neocambrica	MOLLUGINACEAE	Mischarytera lautereriana	SAPINDACEAE
Macroptilium atropurpureum	FABACEAE	Mischocarpus australis	SAPINDACEAE
Macrozamia douglasii	ZAMIACEAE	Mischocarpus pyriformis subsp. pyriformis	SAPINDACEAE
Macrozamia pauli-guilielmi	ZAMIACEAE	mistflower	ASTERACEAE
maidenhair fern	PTERIDACEAE	mistletoe	LORANTHACEAE
mango bark	BURSERACEAE	Mitrasacme paludosa	LOGANIACEAE
mangrove waxflower vine	APOCYNACEAE	Mitrasacme polymorpha	LOGANIACEAE
many-flowered mat rush	LAXMANNIACEAE	monkey vine	APOCYNACEAE
mare's tail fern	ASPLENIACEAE	Monotoca scoparia	ERICACEAE
marine couch	POACEAE	Monotoca sp.	ERICACEAE
Marsdenia fraseri	APOCYNACEAE	Moreton Bay ash	MYRTACEAE
Marsdenia glandulifera	APOCYNACEAE	morinda	RUBIACEAE
Marsdenia rostrata	APOCYNACEAE	morning glory	CONVOLVULACEAE
marsh wort	MENYANTHACEAE	mort's dockrillia	ORCHIDACEAE
mat rush	LAXMANNIACEAE	mosquito orchid	ORCHIDACEAE
Mcdonald's laurel	LAURACEAE	Mossman River grass	POACEAE
medicine bush	RUBIACEAE	moth bladderwort	LENTIBULARIACEAE
Medicosma cunninghamii	RUTACEAE	mouse ear chickweed	CAROPHYLLACEAE
Melaleuca dealbata	MYRTACEAE	Mucuna gigantea	FABACEAE
Melaleuca nodosa	MYRTACEAE	Muellerina bidwillii	LORANTHACEAE

Muellerina celastroides	LORANTHACEAE
Myoporum acuminatum	SCROPHULARIACEAE
Myoporum boninense subsp. *australe*	SCROPHULARIACEAE
Myriophyllum implicatum	HALORAGACEAE
Myrsine arenaria	MYRSINACEAE
Myrsine subsessilis subsp. *subsessilis*	MYRSINACEAE
Myrsine variabilis	MYRSINACEAE
myrtle mangrove	MYRTACEAE
narrow -leafed gardenia	RUBIACEAE
narrow leafed geebung	PROTEACEAE
narrow-leaf carpet grass	POACEAE
narrow-leaf platysace	APIACEAE
narrow-leafed milk vine	APOCYNACEAE
native bleeding heat	EUPHORBIACEAE
native celtis	ULMACEAE
native cherry	SANTALACEAE
native cobbler's peggs	ASTERACEAE
native ginger	ZINGIBERACEAE
native hydrangea	CARPODETACEAE
native iris	IRIDACEAE
native sarsaparilla vine	FABACEAE
native sea lavender	PLUMBAGINACEAE
native violet	VIOLACEAE
native wisteria	FABACEAE
native yam	DIOSCOREACEAE
needlebark stringybark	MYRTACEAE
Neolitsea dealbata	LAURACEAE
Nephrolepis cordifolia	LOMARIOPSIDACEAE
netted bracken	PTERIDACEAE
netted yellow wood	RUTACEAE
New Zealand spinach	AIZOACEAE
nicker bean	CAESALPINIACEAE
nodding greenhood	ORCHIDACEAE
nodding greenhood orchid	ORCHIDACEAE
noon flower	AIZOACEAE
northern buttonwood	MYRSINACEAE
northern evodia	RUTACEAE
northern guioa	SAPINDACEAE
Notelaea longifolia forma *glabra*	OLEACEAE

Notelaea punctata	OLEACEAE
Notothixos subaureus	VISCACEAE
Nymphaea caerulea	NYMPHAECEAE
Nymphoides exiliflora	MENYANTHACEAE
Oberonia complanata	ORCHIDACEAE
Oberonia palmicola	ORCHIDACEAE
Ochrosperma lineare	MYRTACEAE
Oenothera affinis	ONAGRACEAE
Oenothera drummondii subsp. *drummondii*	ONAGRACEAE
olax	OLEACEAE
Olax retusa	OLEACEAE
oliver's sassafras	LAURACEAE
Ophioglossum pendulum	OPHIOGLOSSACEAE
Oplismenus aemulus	POACEAE
Oplismenus imbecillis	POACEAE
Oplismenus mollis	POACEAE
Opuntia stricta	CACTACEAE
orange mangrove	RHIZOPHORACEAE
Ornduffia reniformis	MENYANTHACEAE
Osbornia octodonta	MYRTACEAE
Oxalis corniculata	OXALIDACEAE
Oxalis perennans	OXALIDACEAE
Oxalis pes-caprae	OXALIDACEAE
Oxalis rubens	OXALIDACEAE
pale flax lilly	HEMEROCALLIDACEAE
pale sundew	DROSERACEAE
Pandanus tectorius	PANDANACEAE
Pandorea floribunda	BIGNONIACEAE
Pandorea jasminoides	BIGNONIACEAE
panic grass	POACEAE
Panicum effusum	POACEAE
Panicum lachnophyllum	POACEAE
Panicum simile	POACEAE
para grass	POACEAE
Paracaleana minor	ORCHIDACEAE
Paramatta grass	POACEAE
Parsonsia latifolia	APOCYNACEAE
Parsonsia straminea	APOCYNACEAE
Parsonsia velutina	APOCYNACEAE
Parsonsia ventricosa	APOCYNACEAE

Paspalidium constrictum	POACEAE	pig face	AIZOACEAE
Paspalidium gausum	POACEAE	*Pilidiostigma glabrum*	MYRTACEAE
Paspalidium gracile	POACEAE	*Pimelea linifolia*	THYMELAEACEAE
Paspalum conjugatum	POACEAE	*Pimelea linifolia* subsp. *linifolia*	THYMELAEACEAE
Paspalum dilatatum	POACEAE	pin flower tree	PHYLLANTHACEAE
Paspalum mandiocanum	POACEAE	pink ash	RHAMNACEAE
Paspalum scrobiculatum	POACEAE	pink bloodwood	MYRTACEAE
Paspalum vaginatum	POACEAE	pink fingers	ORCHIDACEAE
Passiflora edulis	PASSIFLORACEAE	pink flowered evodia	RUTACEAE
Passiflora suberosa	PASSIFLORACEAE	pink heart	RUTACEAE
pastal flower	ACANTHACEAE	pink nodding orchid	ORCHIDACEAE
Patersonia glabrata	IRIDACEAE	pink trumpet flower	CONVOLVULACEAE
Patersonia sericea var. *sericea*	IRIDACEAE	pink wax flower	RUTACEAE
pea flower	FABACEAE	*Piper caninum*	PIPERACEAE
pearl bearded heath	ERICACEAE	*Piper hederaceum* var.	PIPERACEAE
pennywort	APIACEAE	*hederaceum*	
pepper vine	PIPERACEAE	pipewort	ERIOCAULACEAE
Peristeranthus hillii	ORCHIDACEAE	*Pitaviaster haplophyllus*	RUTACEAE
Persea americana	LAURACEAE	pithy swod sedge	CYPERACEAE
Persicaria orientalis	POLYGONACEAE	pitted-leaf steelwood	SAPINDACEAE
Persoonia media	PROTEACEAE	*Pittosporum revolutum*	PITTOSPORACEAE
Persoonia prostrata	PROTEACEAE	*Pityrogramma calomelanos* var.	PTERIDACEAE
Persoonia stradbrokensis	PROTEACEAE	*austroamericana*	
Persoonia tenuifolia	PROTEACEAE	pixie caps	ORCHIDACEAE
Persoonia virgata	PROTEACEAE	*Planchonella australis*	SAPOTACEAE
Petalostigma pubescens	PICRODENRACEAE	*Planchonella chartacea*	SAPOTACEAE
Petrophile shirleyae	PROTEACEAE	*Planchonia careya*	LECYTHIDACEAE
Phaius australis	ORCHIDACEAE	*Plantago lanceolata*	PLANTAGINACEAE
phaleria	THYMELAEACEAE	*Platycerium bifurcatum*	POLYPODIACEAE
Phaleria chermsideana	THYMELAEACEAE	*Platycerium superbum*	POLYPODIACEAE
Phaleria octandra	THYMELAEACEAE	*Platylobium formosum*	FABACEAE
Phebalium woombye	RUTACEAE	*Platysace ericoides*	APIACEAE
Philydrum lanuginosum	PHILYDRACEAE	*Platysace lanceolata*	APIACEAE
Phragmites australis	POACEAE	*Platysace linearifolia*	APIACEAE
Phyla nodiflora	VERBENACEAE	*Plectranthus parviflorus*	LAMIACEAE
Phyllanthus tenellus	PHYLLANTHACEAE	*Pleiogynium timorense*	ANACARDIACEAE
Phyllanthus virgatus	PHYLLANTHACEAE	*Pleioluma queenslandica*	SAPOTACEAE
Phyllota phylicoides	FABACEAE	plum myrtle	MYRTACEAE
piccabeen palm	ARECACEAE	*Poa annua*	POACEAE
Picris angustifolia subsp.	ASTERACEAE	*Podocarpus elatus*	PODOCARPACEAE
carolorum-henricorum		*Podolepis arachnoidea*	ASTERACEAE

Podolepis longipedata	ASTERACEAE
Podolepis neglecta	ASTERACEAE
pointed aotus	FABACEAE
pointed silk pod	APOCYNACEAE
pointed-leaf hovea	FABACEAE
poison peach	ULMACEAE
poisonous corkwood	SOLANACEAE
pololepis	ASTERACEAE
Polyalthia nitidissima	ANNONACEAE
Polycarpon tetraphyllum	CAROPHYLLACEAE
Polymeria calycina	CONVOLVULACEAE
Polyscias australiana	ARALIACEAE
Polyscias elegans	ARALIACEAE
Pomax umbellata	RUBIACEAE
poor man's gold	FABACEAE
Poranthera microphylla	PHYLLANTHACEAE
Portulaca pilosa	PORTULACEAE
potato weed	ASTERACEAE
pouched coral fern	GLEICHENIACEAE
poverty grass	POACEAE
prairie grass	POACEAE
Prasophyllum brevilabre	ORCHIDACEAE
Prasophyllum exilis	ORCHIDACEAE
Praxelis clematidea	ASTERACEAE
prickly broom heath	ERICACEAE
prickly couch	POACEAE
prickly guinea flower	DILLENIACEAE
prickly moses	MIMOSACEAE
prickly paperbark	MYRTACEAE
prickly supplejack	RIPOGONACEAE
prickly tea-tree	MYRTACEAE
prickly tree fern	CYATHEACEAE
princes feathers	POLYGONACEAE
Pseudanthus orientalis	PICRODENRACEAE
Pseuderanthemum variabile	ACANTHACEAE
Pseudognaphalium luteoalbum	ASTERACEAE
Pseudoraphis paradoxa	POACEAE
Psilotum nudum	PSILOTACEAE
Psychotria daphnoides	RUBIACEAE
Psychotria loniceroides	RUBIACEAE

Psydrax lamprophylla forma *lamprophylla*	RUBIACEAE
Pteridium esculentum	DENNSTAEDTIACEAE
Pteridoblechnum neglectum	BLECHNACEAE
Pteris comans	PTERIDACEAE
Pterocaulon redolens	ASTERACEAE
Pterostylis acuminata	ORCHIDACEAE
Pterostylis antennifera	ORCHIDACEAE
Pterostylis baptistii	ORCHIDACEAE
Pterostylis erecta	ORCHIDACEAE
Pterostylis hispidula	ORCHIDACEAE
Pterostylis nigricans	ORCHIDACEAE
Pterostylis nutans	ORCHIDACEAE
Pterostylis ophioglossa	ORCHIDACEAE
Pterostylis parviflora	ORCHIDACEAE
Pterostylis revoluta	ORCHIDACEAE
Pultenaea euchila	FABACEAE
Pultenaea rarifolia	FABACEAE
Pultenaea robusta	FABACEAE
Pultenaea villosa	FABACEAE
purple bush pea	FABACEAE
purpletop chloris	POACEAE
Pyrrosia rupestris	POLYPODIACEAE
Qld blue couch	POACEAE
queen of the bush	THYMELAEACEAE
quinine tree	PICRODENRACEAE
rapania	MYRSINACEAE
raspwort	HALORAGACEAE
raspy root orchid	ORCHIDACEAE
rats tail grass	POACEAE
rattlepod	FABACEAE
red ash	RHAMNACEAE
red bloodwood	MYRTACEAE
red buttonwood	MYRSINACEAE
red cedar	MELIACEAE
red honeysuckle	PROTEACEAE
red mahogany	MYRTACEAE
red mistletoe	LORANTHACEAE
red Natal grass	POACEAE
red pear fruit	SAPINDACEAE
red rope orchid	ORCHIDACEAE

red-head cottonbush	APOCYNACEAE	*Schoenoplectus tabernaemontani*	CYPERACEAE
Rhinerrhiza divitiflora	ORCHIDACEAE	*Schoenus apogon* var. *apogon*	CYPERACEAE
Rhizophora mucronata	RHIZOPHORACEAE	*Schoenus brevifolius*	CYPERACEAE
Rhizophora stylosa	RHIZOPHORACEAE	*Schoenus calostachyus*	CYPERACEAE
Rhodamnia acuminata	MYRTACEAE	*Schoenus melanostachys*	CYPERACEAE
Rhodamnia dumicola	MYRTACEAE	*Schoenus nitens*	CYPERACEAE
rhodes grass	POACEAE	*Schoenus ornithopodioides*	CYPERACEAE
ribbon fern	OPHIOGLOSSACEAE	*Schoenus paludosus*	CYPERACEAE
ribbon wood	ANACARDIACEAE	*Schoenus scabripes*	CYPERACEAE
ribbonweed	HYDROCHARITACEAE	*Scolopia braunii*	FLACOURTACEAE
ribwort plantain	PLANTAGINACEAE	*Scoparia dulcis*	SCROPHULARIACEAE
rice flower	THYMELAEACEAE	scrambling berry	HEMEROCALLIDACEAE
Richardia brasiliensis	RUBIACEAE	scrambling coral fern	GLEICHENIACEAE
Ricinocarpos pinifolius	EUPHORBIACEAE	scribbly gum	MYRTACEAE
rifle grass	CYPERACEAE	scrub cherry	MYRTACEAE
Ripogonum discolor	RIPOGONACEAE	scrub daphne	THYMELAEACEAE
river mangrove	MYRSINACEAE	scrub wonga vine	BIGNONIACEAE
rock boronia	RUTACEAE	scurvy weed	COMMELINACEAE
rock felt fern	POLYPODIACEAE	sea bind weed	CONVOLVULACEAE
rough maidenhair fern	PTERIDACEAE	sea celery	APIACEAE
round-leaf goodenia	GOODENIACEAE	sea grass	CYMODOCEACEAE
rubber vine	APOCYNACEAE	sea purslane	AIZOACEAE
runing marsh flower	MENYANTHACEAE	sea rocket	BRASSICACEAE
rush	JUNCACEAE	sea rush	JUNCACEAE
rush lilly	JOHNSONIACEAE	seablite	CHENOPODIACEAE
safron heart	RUTACEAE	sedge	RESTIONACEAE
salt water couch	POACEAE	sedge	CYPERACEAE
samphire	CHENOPODIACEAE	*Selaginella uliginosa*	SELAGINELLACEAE
sandpaper fig	MORACEAE	*Senecio pinnatifolius* var.	ASTERACEAE
Sannantha bidwillii	MYRTACEAE	*pinnatifolius*	
Sarcomelicope simplicifolia subsp.	RUTACEAE	*Senna pendula* var. *glabrata*	CAESALPINACEAE
simplicifolia		*Sesbania cannabina* var.	FABACEAE
Sarcopetalum harveyanum	MENISPERMACEAE	*cannabina*	
Sarcopteryx stipata	SAPINDACEAE	*Sesuvium portulacastrum*	AIZOACEAE
sasparilla vine	SMILACACEAE	*Setaria sphacelata*	POACEAE
Scaevola calendulacea	GOODENIACEAE	*Setaria surgens*	POACEAE
scentless rosewood	MELIACEAE	settler's flax	ARECEAE
Schenkia australis	GENTIANACEAE	sharp greenhood	ORCHIDACEAE
Schizachyrium fragile	POACEAE	sheep sorrel	POLYGONACEAE
Schizaea bifida	SCHIZAEACEAE	shiny bogrush	CYPERACEAE
Schizomeria ovata	CUNONIACEAE	short-lip leek orchid	ORCHIDACEAE

162

showy guinea flower	DILLENIACEAE	smooth clerodendrum	LAMIACEAE
showy parrot pea	FABACEAE	smooth psychotria	RUBIACEAE
shrubby platysace	APIACEAE	smooth-barked apple	MYRTACEAE
sickle wattle	MIMOSACEAE	snake fern	SCHIZAEACEAE
Sida cordifolia	MALVACEAE	snake flower	ORCHIDACEAE
Sida rhombifolia	MALVACEAE	snake tongue greenhood	ORCHIDACEAE
sida-retusa	MALVACEAE	snake vine	DILLENIACEAE
Sigesbeckia orientalis	ASTERACEAE	soft kharkiweed	AMARANTHACEAE
signal grass	POACEAE	soft twigrush	CYPERACEAE
Silene gallica	CAROPHYLLACEAE	*Solanum nigrum* subsp. *nigrum*	SOLANACEAE
silver aspen	RUTACEAE	*Solanum nodiflorum*	SOLANACEAE
silver hair grass	POACEAE	soldiers crest orchid	ORCHIDACEAE
Singapore daisy	ASTERACEAE	*Soliva sessilis*	ASTERACEAE
siratro	FABACEAE	*Sonchus oleraceus*	ASTERACEAE
Sisyrinchium rosulatum	IRIDACEAE	sorrel	OXALIDACEAE
skeleton fork fern	PSILOTACEAE	sour current bush	SANTALACEAE
slender clubmoss	LYCOPODIACEAE	sour grass	POACEAE
slender mudgrass	POACEAE	South African pigeon grass	POACEAE
slender onion orchid	ORCHIDACEAE	South African waterlilly	NYMPHAEACEAE
slender orchid	ORCHIDACEAE	South Qld kauri pine	ARAUCARIACEAE
slender panic	POACEAE	southern salwood	MIMOSACEAE
slender stackhousia	STACKHOUSIACEAE	southern silky oak	PROTEACEAE
slender vervain	VERBENACEAE	*Sowerbaea juncea*	LAXMANNIACEAE
slender wire lilly	LAXMANNIACEAE	*Spermacoce brachystema*	RUBIACEAE
small bladderwort	LENTIBULARIACEAE	*Spermacoce multicaulis*	RUBIACEAE
small bolwarra	EUPOMATIACEAE	*Sphaeromorphaea australis*	ASTERACEAE
small chloanthes	LAMIACEAE	*Sphagneticola trilobata*	ASTERACEAE
small duck orchid	ORCHIDACEAE	spider orchid	ORCHIDACEAE
small flower	POACEAE	spike centaury	GENTIANACEAE
small matweed	AMARANTHACEAE	spike rush	CYPERACEAE
small mosquito orchid	ORCHIDACEAE	*Spinifex sericeus*	POACEAE
small poranthera	PHYLLANTHACEAE	spoon leaved sundew	DROSERACEAE
small St Johns wort	CLUSIACEAE	*Sporadanthus caudata*	RESTIONACEAE
small wasp orchid	ORCHIDACEAE	*Sporadanthus interruptus*	RESTIONACEAE
small waxlip orchid	ORCHIDACEAE	*Sporobolus africanus*	POACEAE
small-leaved fig	MORACEAE	*Sporobolus fertilis*	POACEAE
small-leaved geebung	PROTEACEAE	*Sporobolus laxus*	POACEAE
small-leaved lilly pilly	MYRTACEAE	*Sporobolus virginicus*	POACEAE
small-leaved Moreton Bay fig	MORACEAE	spotted leaved red mangrove	RHIZOPHORACEAE
Smilax australis	SMILACACEAE	spreading nutheads	ASTERACEAE
Smilax glyciphylla	SMILACACEAE	spreading rope rush	RESTIONACEAE

spreading tree fern	GLEICHENIACEAE
sprengela	ERICACEAE
Sprengelia sprengelioides	ERICACEAE
St Augustine grass	POACEAE
Stackhousia spathulata	STACKHOUSIACEAE
Stackhousia viminea	STACKHOUSIACEAE
staghorn	POLYPODIACEAE
star burr	ASTERACEAE
star hair brush	ARALIACEAE
steelwood	SAPINDACEAE
Stellaria media	CAROPHYLLACEAE
Stenotaphrum secundatum	POACEAE
Stephania japonica var. *discolor*	MENISPERMACEAE
Sticherus flabellatus var. *flabellatus*	GLEICHENIACEAE
Sticherus lobatus	GLEICHENIACEAE
sticky hop bush	SAPINDACEAE
stinking cryptocarya	LAURACEAE
straggly baeckea	MYRTACEAE
straggly pencil orchid	ORCHIDACEAE
strand sedge	CYPERACEAE
strangea	PROTEACEAE
Strangea linearis	PROTEACEAE
strangler fig	MORACEAE
streaked arrowgrass	JUNCAGINACEAE
streaked rattlepod	FABACEAE
stringy bark cypress pine	CUPRESSACEAE
Stylidium graminifolium	STYLIDACEAE
Stylidium ornatum	STYLIDACEAE
Stylidium tenerum	STYLIDACEAE
Stylosanthes humilis	FABACEAE
Styphelia viridis subsp. *breviflora*	ERICACEAE
Suaeda arbusculoides	CHENOPODIACEAE
Suaeda australis	CHENOPODIACEAE
summer grass	POACEAE
sundew	DROSERACEAE
sunflower	ASTERACEAE
swamp oak	CASUARINACEAE
swamp barnyard grass	POACEAE
swamp boronia	RUTACEAE
swamp box	MYRTACEAE
swamp grass tree	XANTHORRHOEACEAE

swamp hibiscus	MALVACEAE
swamp lilly	AMARYLLIDACEAE
swamp mahogany	MYRTACEAE
swamp may	MYRTACEAE
swamp orchid	ORCHIDACEAE
swamp paperbark	MYRTACEAE
swamp rice grass	POACEAE
swamp selaginella	SELAGINELLACEAE
swamp tee tree	MYRTACEAE
sweet mitrewort	LOGANIACEAE
sweet susie	RUBIACEAE
sweet wattle	MIMOSACEAE
sword grass	CYPERACEAE
sword sedge	CYPERACEAE
Symphyotrichum subulatum	ASTERACEAE
Symplocos stawellii	SYMPLOCACEAE
Syncarpia hillii	MYRTACEAE
Synoum glandulosum subsp. *glandulosum*	MELIACEAE
Syzygium australe	MYRTACEAE
Syzygium johnsonii	MYRTACEAE
Syzygium luehmannii	MYRTACEAE
Syzygium oleosum	MYRTACEAE
Taeniophyllum muelleri	ORCHIDACEAE
tailed helmut orchid	ORCHIDACEAE
tall baeckea	MYRTACEAE
tall copper-wired daisy	ASTERACEAE
tall fleabane	ASTERACEAE
tall ground berry	ERICACEAE
tall spike rush	CYPERACEAE
tall sword grass	CYPERACEAE
tallowwood	MYRTACEAE
tape fern	PTERIDACEAE
tape vine	MENISPERMACEAE
Tasmannia insipida	WINTERACEAE
tassle rope rush	RESTIONACEAE
Tecomanthe hillii	BIGNONIACEAE
Tecticornia halocnemoides	CHENOPODIACEAE
Tecticornia indica subsp. *leiostachya*	CHENOPODIACEAE
Tephrosia filipes subsp. *filipes*	FABACEAE

Tetragonia tetragonoides	AIZOACEAE	*Utricularia bifida*	LENTIBULARIACEAE
Tetratheca thymifolia	ELAEOCARPACEAE	*Utricularia biloba*	LENTIBULARIACEAE
Thelymitra ixioides	ORCHIDACEAE	*Utricularia caerulea*	LENTIBULARIACEAE
Thelymitra purpurata	ORCHIDACEAE	*Utricularia gibba*	LENTIBULARIACEAE
Themeda triandra	POACEAE	*Utricularia lateriflora*	LENTIBULARIACEAE
thickhead	ASTERACEAE	*Utricularia uliginosa*	LENTIBULARIACEAE
thin-leaved coondoo	SAPOTACEAE	*Vallisneria nana*	HYDROCHARITACEAE
Thysanotus tuberosus subsp. *tuberosus*	LAXMANNIACEAE	vanilla lilly	LAXMANNIACEAE
		variable bossieea	FABACEAE
timonius	RUBIACEAE	variable groundsel	ASTERACEAE
Timonius timon var. *timon*	RUBIACEAE	varied mitrewort	LOGANIACEAE
tiny greenhood	ORCHIDACEAE	veiny morinda	RUBIACEAE
tiny wattle	MIMOSACEAE	veiny wilkiea	MONIMIACEAE
Tmesipteris truncata	PSILOTACEAE	*Velleia spathulata*	GOODENIACEAE
Todea barbara	OSMUNDACEAE	velvet bean	FABACEAE
Toechima tenax	SAPINDACEAE	*Verbena rigida*	VERBENACEAE
tongue orchid	ORCHIDACEAE	vernonia	ASTERACEAE
Toona ciliata	MELIACEAE	*Vigna luteola*	FABACEAE
toothed wattle	MIMOSACEAE	*Vigna marina*	FABACEAE
Townsville stylo	FABACEAE	*Viola hederacea*	VIOLACEAE
Trachymene incisa subsp. *incisa*	ARALIACEAE	Virginian peppercress	BRASSICACEAE
Trachystylis stradbrokensis	CYPERACEAE	*Viscum articulatum*	VISCACEAE
tree bearded heath	ERICACEAE	vitex	LAMIACEAE
tree heath	ERICACEAE	*Vitex trifolia* var. *trifolia*	LAMIACEAE
Trema tomentosa var. *aspera*	ULMACEAE	*Vulpia bromoides*	POACEAE
Tricoryne elatior	JOHNSONIACEAE	*Wahlenbergia stricta*	CAMPANULACEAE
Tricoryne muricata	JOHNSONIACEAE	walking stick palm	ARECACEAE
trigger plant	STYLIDACEAE	wallum banksia	PROTEACEAE
Triglochin striata	JUNCAGINACEAE	wallum bearded heath	ERICACEAE
Trochocarpa laurina	ERICACEAE	wallum boronia	RUTACEAE
Trophis scandens subsp. *scandens*	MORACEAE	wallum bottlebrush	MYRTACEAE
tropical clematis	RANUNCULACEAE	wallum dogwood	FABACEAE
tuckeroo	SAPINDACEAE	wallum hakea	PROTEACEAE
tulipwood	SAPINDACEAE	wallum heath	ERICACEAE
twiggy homoranthus	MYRTACEAE	wallum leek orchid	ORCHIDACEAE
twigrush	CYPERACEAE	wallum mat rush	LAXMANNIACEAE
twining glycine	FABACEAE	wallum sun orchid	ORCHIDACEAE
two colour panic	POACEAE	wallum tea-tree	MYRTACEAE
umbrella tree fern	GLEICHENIACEAE	wallum wedge pea	FABACEAE
Urochloa decumbens	POACEAE	wallum woombye	RUTACEAE
Urochloa distachya	POACEAE	wallum zieria	RUTACEAE
Urochloa mutica	POACEAE	wanderrie grass	POACEAE

water fern	THELYPTERIDACEAE	wonga wonga vine	BIGNONIACEAE
water milfoil	HALORAGACEAE	woody pear	PROTEACEAE
water-ribbons	JUNCAGINACEAE	*Woollsia pungens*	ERICACEAE
wattle	MIMOSACEAE	woolly glycine	FABACEAE
wedding bush	EUPHORBIACEAE	woolly water lilly	PHILYDRACEAE
weeping love grass	POACEAE	woolsia	ERICACEAE
weeping myrtle	MYRTACEAE	wooly tea-tree	MYRTACEAE
whip vine	FLAGELLARIACEAE	wooly xanthosia	APIACEAE
whire myrtle	MYRTACEAE	wormseed	CHENOPODIACEAE
whiskey grass	POACEAE	*Xanthorrhoea fulva*	XANTHORRHOEACEAE
white beech	LAMIACEAE	*Xanthorrhoea johnsonii*	XANTHORRHOEACEAE
white bolly gum	LAURACEAE	*Xanthorrhoea macronema*	XANTHORRHOEACEAE
white caladenia	ORCHIDACEAE	*Xanthosia pilosa*	APIACEAE
white cedar	MELIACEAE	*Xerochrysum bracteatum*	ASTERACEAE
white cypress pine	CUPRESSACEAE	*Xylocarpus granatum*	MELIACEAE
white donkey orchid	ORCHIDACEAE	*Xylomelum benthamii*	PROTEACEAE
white elipta	ASTERACEAE	*Xyris complanata*	XYRIDACEAE
white eye	RUBIACEAE	*Xyris juncea*	XYRIDACEAE
white hazelwood	SYMPLOCACEAE	*Xyris operculata*	XYRIDACEAE
white karambal	ACANTHACEAE	yam	VITACEAE
white root	CAMPANULACEAE	yellow ash	RHAMNACEAE
white sandpaper fig	MORACEAE	yellow aspen	RUTACEAE
white siris	SIMAROUBACEAE	yellow buttons	ASTERACEAE
white sour bush	SANTALACEAE	yellow eclipta	ASTERACEAE
Wide Bay boronia	RUTACEAE	yellow eye	XYRIDACEAE
Wide Bay hovea	FABACEAE	yellow mangrove	RHIZOPHORACEAE
Wikstroemia indica	THYMELAEACEAE	yellow pea bush	FABACEAE
wild aster	ASTERACEAE	yellow pear fruit	SAPINDACEAE
wild ginger	ZINGIBERACEAE	yellow rush lilly	JOHNSONIACEAE
wild may	MYRTACEAE	yellow sorrel	OXALIDACEAE
wild pansies	GOODENIACEAE	yellow stringybark	MYRTACEAE
wild parsnip	ARALIACEAE	yellow tea-tree	MYRTACEAE
wild pea	FABACEAE	zamia palm	ZAMIACEAE
wild quince	SAPINDACEAE	*Zeuxine oblonga*	ORCHIDACEAE
Wilkiea huegeliana	MONIMIACEAE	*Zieria laxiflora*	RUTACEAE
Wilkiea macrophylla	MONIMIACEAE	*Zieria smithii*	RUTACEAE
willow guinea flower	DILLENIACEAE	zig zag vine	ANNONACEAE
winged-leaved tulipwood	SAPINDACEAE	*Zornia dyctiocarpa* var.	FABACEAE
wire grass	POACEAE	*dyctiocarpa*	
wiry panic	POACEAE	*Zoysia macrantha* subsp.	POACEAE
Wollastonia uniflora	ASTERACEAE	*macrantha*	
wombat berry	LAXMANNIACEAE		

GLOSSARY

A horizon	top layer of the soil horizon, or 'topsoil' which contains dark decomposed organic matter, called "humus"
m a.s.l.	metres above sea level
Aquatic Herb	herbs that have adapted to living in aquatic environments (saltwater or freshwater)
B horizon	referred to as the 'subsoil' and the zone of accumulation where rainwater percolating through the soil has leached material from above and it has precipitated within the B horizon, often giving it an orange colour
Basalt dykes	formed when molten magma flows upward through near-vertical cracks (faults or joints) toward the surface and cools
Biomass	the total quantity or weight (expressed as oven dry-weight) of plants in a given area
Broad Vegetation Groups (BVGs)	are a high-level groupings of vegetation communities developed by the Queensland Herbarium
Cherts	hard, fine-grained sedimentary rock composed of very small crystals of quartz
Cretaceous organic sand	mass of fine siliceous sand and its decomposing organic material which results in impervious organically bound sand
Cretaceous Period	Cretaceous is a geological period that lasted from about 145 to 66 million years ago
Endemic	having a natural distribution confined to a particular geographical region

Epiphyte	plant living on another plant but not obtaining nourishment from that plant e.g. an orchid
Fens	short word of Germanic origin for Fenna, Fenne, Frederike, Fredenand, and Fridenand which means wetland with neutral, or only slightly acid peaty soil
Fore Dune	dunes situated immediately behind the Strand and are up to 20 m in height. These dunes include the second berm and larger seepage areas such as swales creeks and lagoons
Fraser Island / K'gari	Fraser Island / K'gari was officially recognised under provisions of the Act on 1 July 2011 along with a number of geographical features on the island. Under current alternative naming principles, the island is known officially as Fraser Island / K'gari. The Traditional Owners, the Butchulla People refer to the island as K'gari, pronounced as Gari. The alternative name, Gari comes from the Badtjala Language for Fraser Island. (Badtjala Word List by Wondunna Aboriginal Corporation 1996 Page 160)
Genus	group (pl. Genera)
Herb	plant with non-woody stem
High Dune	much of the central part of the island above 80 m which contain most of the better developed forests including the *Eucalyptus pilularis* (blackbutt) dominated forests, 'satinay-brush box forests' and rainforests (closed forest)
High Water Springs	this is the tide which occurs approximately once a fortnight when the range of tide is greatest, during the full and new moon
Hind Dune	parabolic dunes (with a trailing edge) which extend up to a height of 80 m in height and up to three kilometres inland - soils are usually yellow/brown with little organic matter in the surface layers

Holocene Period	a geological epoch which began at the end of the Pleistocene Period (at 11,700 calendar years Before Present) and continues to the present
Humus podzols	soils with high content of organic matter and appreciable amounts of extractable iron
Ice Age	most recent ice age occurred in the Pleistocene about 2.6 million years ago and lasted until about 11,700 years ago
Littoral Flats	area that are of or on the shore, area lying along the western shore
Mangrove	a tree or shrub which grows in tidal, chiefly tropical, coastal swamps, having numerous tangled roots that grow above ground and form dense thickets
Mesozoic Era	spans from about 252 million years ago to about 66 million years ago, when giant reptiles, dinosaurs and other monstrous beasts roamed the world
Myrtaceae	the myrtle family of shrubs and trees containing about 150 genera and 3,300 species that are widely distributed in the tropics and have rather leathery evergreen leaves with oil glands
Nett primary production	amount of carbon and energy that enters ecosystems and provides the energy that drives all biotic processes, including the decomposer organisms that recycle the nutrients required to support primary production
Palaeozoic Era	from about 542 million years ago to 251 million years ago, was a time of great change on the Earth, with the formation of the continents
Palm	an unbranched evergreen tree of tropical and warm regions, with a crown of very long feathered or fan-shaped leaves, and typically having old leaf scars forming a regular pattern on the trunk
Parasitic Shrub	a shrub living on another plant and obtaining nourishment from the host plant

Parasitic Vine	vine form of a parasitic plant which take nutrients and water from other plants by extracting them from their host's roots, stems, branches, and sometimes leaves
Peat (organic soil)	a brown organic soil made up of partially-decomposed plant material of acid-loving plants, which have built up over about 10,000 years in poorly-drained wetland habitats, often referred to as bogs and fens
Physiography	the physical characteristics of the area more generally describing the physical processes or forces that formed the landscape
Pleistocene Period	lasted from about 2,580,000 to 11,700 years ago, spanning the world's most recent period of repeated glaciations
Quartzose sand	contains more than 90% quartz
Rainforests	closed forests that have dense canopies (70-100 % cover) in the upper level, that allows little sunlight to penetrate to lower levels. There is no universally agreed definition, but a strong consensus position which focuses on features such as a closed evergreen canopy; contains trees 25 m tall or higher; abundant epiphytes; the presence of large, thick-stemmed woody climbers (vines); warm, wet, and relatively aseasonal climate
Rhizomatous Herb	herb with a horizontal creeping underground soft stem which can send out roots
Sand podzols	soils with an ash-grey subsurface horizon, on top of a dark horizon with brown or black humus and/or reddish iron compounds
Sclerophyll	a type of vegetation that has hard leaves with short internodes (the distance between leaves along the stem) and leaf orientation parallel or oblique to direct sunlight
Shrub	woody plant less than 5 m high, usually with more than one stem arising from near ground level

Species	able to interbreed, specific group of closely related individuals with small differences or variations and usually written as '*species*' sp. refers to a plant in a genus when the species is not known spp. refers collectively to some or all, of the species in a genus
Strand	area comprising beach and dune sands and extends from the high water mark up to a height of approximately 5 m and includes the first berm (sand ridge) and small seepage areas above the high-water mark
Succulent Herb	plants with fleshy parts, such as leaves, stems or trunks
Swale	a shady spot, or a sunken or marshy place
Trachyte	an igneous volcanic rock
Transgressive Sand Dune	are relatively large-scale wind-blown sand deposits formed by the downwind and/or alongshore movement of sand over vegetated to semi-vegetated areas
Tree	woody plant more than 5 m high with usually one stem
Tree Fern	a fern that grows with a trunk with the fronds above ground level
Tufted Herb	a herb with one or more groups of short branches all arising from the same level
Vine	a climbing or trailing woody-stemmed plant
Wallum	name given to some species of Banksia by the aborigines of south-eastern Queensland, and the term 'wallum' has been adopted for low lying areas of coastal sandy acid soils where these plants are common
Xeromorphic	a species of plant that has morphological and physiological adaptations to enable it to survive in an environment with little liquid water

ACKNOWLEDGEMENTS

The provision of unpublished information from the Queensland Department of Forestry revegetation research on sand-mined areas is gratefully appreciated.

The author warmly acknowledges James Elsol for his early contribution to some of the vegetation descriptions and collection of samples when a member of the Queensland Herbarium.

I would particularly like to thank Laurie Jessup, Bill McDonald and Gordon Guymer, from the Queensland Herbarium, who at the start of this project provided a great deal of technical support. Over the years they have encouraged me to publish the list of species and consistently aided with the preparation of the vegetation descriptions and the identification of the plant species in the field and from herbarium records.

I would like to acknowledge the late Professor Bryant Richards from the University of New England and thank Dr Ian Bevege from the Queensland Forestry Department (as it was known then), for providing me the opportunity to undertake the research on Fraser Island. This enabled me to explore much of the island and gain a greater appreciation of the vegetation along with its natural beauty.

Thanks to Beryl Robertson who kindly gave me copyright permission to use the beautiful painting of *Banksia robur* which embellishes the cover of the book.

I would like to thank Bramita Andriana from petiterabbit.com for her willingness to undertake the design, layout and preparation of the drawings which she did not only with great skill but with thoughtful encouragement and willingness to resolve the numerous issues which arose.

REFERENCES

1. State Government of Queensland. *Commission of Inquiry into the Conservation, Management and Use of Fraser Island and the Great Sandy Region. Initial Discussion Paper.* (1990).

2. Thom B.G. Chappell J. Holocene sea levels relative to Australia. *Search* **6 (3)**, 90–93 (1975).

3. Whitehouse F.W. Fraser Island - geology and geomorphology. *Queensland Naturalist* **19 (1–3)**, 3–9 (1968).

4. BOM (Bureau of Meteorology). Summary Rainfall Records for the Sandy Cape Lighthouse, Fraser Island. Available at http://www.bom.gov.au/climate/data. [verified 7 January 2016]. *http://www.bom.gov.au/climate/data.* (2015).

5. Stanton, J. P. *A report on Fraser Island-natural history, land use, land classification, and a proposed framework for its management. Fraser Island Environmental Enquiry. Final report of the Commission of Inquiry. The Parliament of the Commonwealth of Australia. Parliamentary Paper No. 333/1976.* (1975).

6. Ward, W. T. Sand movement on Fraser Island: A response to changing climates. in *Fraser Island Occasional Papers in Anthropology No.8.* 113–126 (1977).

7. Lee-Manwar, G., Arthrington, A.H. and Timms, B. V. Comparative studies of Brown Lake, Tortoise Lagoon and Blue Lake, North Stradbroke Island, Queensland. Morphometry and origin of the lakes. *Proceedings of the Royal Society of Queensland* **91**, 53–60 (1980).

8. Bayly, I.A.E.; Ebsworth, E. P. and H. F. W. Studies on the lakes of Fraser Island, Queensland. *Australian Journal of Freshwater Research* **26**, 1–13 (1975).

9. Bensink, A.H.A. and Burton, H. A place for freshwater invertebrates. *Proceedings of the Royal Society of Queensland* **86**, 29–45 (1975).

10. Ward, W. T. *Quaternary geology and geomorphology of Fraser Island, in (ed.) R.W. Day: 1977 Field Conference, Lady Elliot Island - Fraser Island-Gayndah-Biggenden. Geological Society of Australia Incorporated, Queensland Division.* (1975).

11. Walker, J., Thompson, C.H., Fergus, I.F., and Tunstall, B. R. Plant succession and soil development in coastal sand dunes of subtropical eastern Australia. in *Forest Succession; Concepts and Application* (1980).

12. James P.M. Notes on the geomorphology of Fraser Island. in *Occasional papers in Anthropology No. 8* 107–111 (1977).

13. Ball, L. C. Report on oil prospecting, near Tewantin. *Queensland Government Mining Journal* **25**, 354–360 (1924).

14. Ward, W.T. and Little, I. P. Times of coastal sand accumulation in south-east Queensland. *Proceedings of the Ecological Society of Australia* **9**, 313–317 (1975).

15. Ward, W.T., Stevens, A.W. and McIntyre, N. *Brisbane's north coast and Fraser Island from the air, in (ed.) R.W. Day: 1977 Field Conference, Lady Elliot Island - Fraser Island-Gayndah-Biggenden.* (1977).

16. Ward, W. T. Correlation of Eastern Australian Pleistocene shorelines with deep-sea core stages: a basis for coastal chronology. *Bulletin Geological Society of America* **96,** 1156–1166 (1985).

17. Bird. E.C.F. Dune stability on Fraser Island. *Queensland Naturalist* **21**, 15–21 (1974).

18. Thompson, C.H. and Ward, W. T. Soil Landscapes of North Stradbroke Island. *Proceedings of the Royal Society of Queensland* **86,** 9–14 (1975).

19. Whitehouse F.W. Wallum country. *Queensland Naturalist* **18**, 64–72 (1967)

20. Specht, R. L. Vegetation. in *The Australian Environment, 4th edition* (1970).

21. Elsol, J. A. E. and Applegate, G. B. Field Trip 14, *Fraser Island XIII Botanical Congress*. (1981).

22. Moss, P., Tibby, J., Shapland, F., Barr, C. and Fairfax, R. *A report into the fire history of the Pattern Fens of the Great Sandy Region, South East Queensland*. (2012).

23. Stewart, P.C.F. and Moss, T. Fire Patterns of South Eastern Queensland in a Global Context: A Review. in *Proceedings of the large wildland fires conference; May 19-23, 2014; Missoula MT* (2014).

24. Longmore, M. E., and Heijnis, H. Aridity in Australia: Pleistocene records of palaeohydrological and palaeoecological change from the perched lake sediments of Fraser Island, Queensland, Australia. *Quaternary International* **57**, 35–47 (1999).

25. Interdepartmental Committee. *Fraser Island Management Plan Report.* (1978).

26. Pryor, L. D. *Biology of Eucalypts. The Institute of Biology's Studies in Biology No. 61.* (1976).

27. Thomas, M. B. and McDonald, W. J. F. *Rare and Threatened Plants of Queensland: A Checklist of geographically Restricted, Poorly Collected and/or Threatened Vascular Plant Species, 2nd edn., Queensland Dept. of Primary Industry, Brisbane.* (1989).

28. Twyford, K. Fraser's newly discovered fens. *MOONMI 89 (Fraser Island Defender's Organisation)* (1996).

29. Sinclair, J. *Discovering Fraser Island & Cooloola.* (1997).

30. Moss, P. Moon Point Mires- a 40,000 year window into Fraser Island Environment. in *6ᵗʰ Biennial Fraser Island Conference, University of the Sunshine Coast, Sippy Downs, QLD, Australia 12 th August 2015* (2015).

31. Moss Patrick, Tibby John, Shapland Felicity, Fairfax Russell, Stewart Philip, Barr Cameron, Petherick Lynda, Gontz Allen, S. C. Patterned fen formation and development from the Great Sandy Region, south-east Queensland, Australia. *Marine and Freshwater Research* **67**, 816–827 (2015).

32. Neldner, V.J., Niehus, R.E., Wilson, B.A., McDonald, W.J.F. and Ford, A. J. *The Vegetation of Queensland. Descriptions of Broad Vegetation Groups.* (2015).

33. Applegate, G. B. Biomass of Blackbutt (*Eucalyptus pilularis*) Forests on Fraser Island. (1982).

34. Powell Judith. *Travel Routes, Forests, Towns and Settlements. Joint Commonwealth and Queensland RFA Steering Committee.* (1998).

35. Queensland Government. *The Conservation, Management and Use of Fraser Island and the Great Sandy Region. Initial Discussion Paper.* (1990).

36. Commonwealth of Australia. *Final Report of the Commission of Inquiry,* Fraser Island Environmental Inquiry, AGPS, Canberra. (1976).

37. Queensland Department of Forestry. *Revegetation Studies on Sand Mined Areas - Fraser Island.* (1979).

38. Florence, R. G. Vegetation pattern in east coast forests. *Linnean Society of N.S.W. Proceedings* **88**, 164–179 (1963).

39. Fisher, W. J. Forest Management Practices on Fraser Island. in *Occasional papers in Anthropology No. 8.* (1977).

40. Taylor, P. *Growing Up- Forestry in Queensland.* (1994).

41. Queensland Government. *Queensland WWII Historic Places. Fraser Commando School, North White Cliffs, Fraser Island.* (2014).

APPENDIX 1

A DESCRIPTION OF THE BVGS FOUND ON FRASER ISLAND

(extract from Neldner et al. 2015).

In 2015, there were 1383 regional ecosystems recognised across Queensland. Regional ecosystems are defined and mapped at 1:100,000 scale across the state. Many regional ecosystems include one or more vegetation communities, some of which are only recognised and mapped at scales larger than 1:100,000.

A vegetation community is an association within a regional ecosystem that has similar structure and floristics and occurs within the same land zone.

Broad Vegetation Groups (BVGs) are a higher-level grouping of vegetation communities and regional ecosystems. BVGs provide an overview of vegetation across the state or a bioregion. They are a useful addition to the regional ecosystem framework by providing an overview of major ecological patterns and relationships across Queensland, independent of bioregions and land zones, and facilitate comparisons with vegetation in other states and internationally [38]. The BVG codes and their descriptions for Fraser Island are as follows:

BVG CODE FOR FRASER ISLAND	DESCRIPTION
35c	Palustrine wetlands. Freshwater swamps on coastal floodplains dominated by sedges and grasses such as *Oryza* spp., *Eleocharis* spp. (spikerush) or *Baloskion* spp. (cord rush) / *Leptocarpus tenax* / *Gahnia sieberiana* (sword grass) / *Lepironia* spp. (land zones 3, 2, 1) (CYP, GUP, BRB, SEQ, WET, [CQC])

BVG CODE FOR FRASER ISLAND	DESCRIPTION
28a	Complex of open shrub land to closed shrubland, grassland, low woodland and open forest, on the Strand and Fore Dune. Includes pure stands of *Casuarina equisetifolia* (coastal sheoak). (land zones 2, 1) (GUP, SEQ, BRB, CYP, [WET, CQC])
9g	Moist to dry woodlands to open forest dominated by stringy barks or mahoganies such as *Eucalyptus tindaliae* (Queensland white stringybark), *E. latisinensis* (white mahogany), *E. acmenoides* (narrow-leaved white stringybark); or *E. racemosa* (scribbly gum) or *E. seeana* or *E. tereticornis* (blue gum) and *Corymbia intermedia* (pink bloodwood). (land zone 5, 12, 9-10, 2, 11, [8, 3]) (SEQ)
8b	Moist open forests to tall open forests mostly dominated by *Eucalyptus pilularis* (Blackbutt) on coastal sands, sub-coastal sandstones and basalt ranges. Also includes tall open forests dominated by *E. montivaga, E. obliqua* (messmate stringybark) and *E. campanulata* (New England ash). (land zones 12, 9, 11, 2, 5, 8) (SEQ, [CQC])
28b	Open forest to woodland dominated by *Acacia crassicarpa* (brown salwood) or other *Acacia* spp. with *Syzygium* spp., *Corymbia* spp. and/or *Parinari nonda* (parinari). (land zones 2, 3, [11]) (CYP, BRB, CQC, WET)
34a	Lacustrine wetlands. Lakes, ephemeral to permanent, fresh to brackish; water bodies with ground water connectivity. Includes fringing woodlands and sedgelands. (land zones 3, 2, [1]) (CHC, DEU, MUL, CYP, BRB, SEQ, [CQC, WET])

BVG CODE FOR FRASER ISLAND	DESCRIPTION
3a	Evergreen to semi-deciduous, notophyll to microphyll vine forest/ thicket on beach ridges and coastal dunes, occasionally *Araucaria cunninghamii* (hoop pine) microphyll vine forest on dunes. *Pisonia grandis* on coral cays. (land zone 2, [5]) (CYP, GUP, SEQ, WET, BRB, CQC) (Tracey 1982 2b)
28a	Complex of open shrubland to closed shrubland, grassland, low woodland and open forest, on strand and fore dune. Includes pure stands of *Casuarina equisetifolia* (coastal sheoak). (land zones 2, 1) (GUP, SEQ, BRB, CYP, [WET, CQC])
29a	Open heaths and dwarf open heaths on coastal dunefields, sandplains and headlands. (land zones 5, 2, 3, 7, 10, [12, 11]) (CYP, SEQ, [WET])
28e	Palustrine wetlands. Sedgelands/grasslands on seeps and soaks on wet peaks, coastal dunes and other non-floodplain features. (land zones 3, 9, 12, [11]) (WET, SEQ, NET, BRB)
35a	Closed forests and low closed forests dominated by mangroves. (land zone 1) (CYP, GUP, BRB, SEQ, WET, CQC)
35b	Bare saltpans ± areas of *Tecticornia* spp. (samphire) sparse forbland and/or *Xerochloa imberbis* or *Sporobolus virginicus* (sand couch) tussock grassland. (land zone 1, [3]) (GUP, BRB, CYP, SEQ, CQC, [WET])